DECORATING EGGS
In the Style of Fabergé

Pamela Purves

DECORATING
❀EGGS❀
In the Style of Fabergé

SEARCH PRESS

First published in Great Britain 1989
Search Press Ltd
Wellwood, North Farm Road,
Tunbridge Wells, Kent TN2 3DR

Editor, Rosalind Dace
Designer, Julie Wood
Photographs by Search Press Studios

The author would like to thank The
Egg Crafters' Guild of Great Britain,
of which she is a member, for
supplying some of the decorations
and accessories illustrated in this
book. She would also like to thank
Pauline for her help and her parents,
Deborah, Gary, June and Gordon,
for letting her borrow their eggs.

ISBN 0 85532 606 9 (c)
ISBN 0 85532 644 1 (pb)

Typeset by Scribe Design,
123 Watling Street, Gillingham,
Kent.
Made and printed in Spain by
Salingraf S.A.L., Bilbao

Contents

The British Protection
of Birds Act 1954
made the taking and selling of
wild birds' eggs illegal. It was updated
in 1982 in the Wildlife and Countryside Act.
This Act states that it is an offence
to take, sell, destroy or have
in one's possession any wild bird's egg.
It is not, however, an offence to own
old eggs collected during Victorian times.
But however intrinsically valuable
an old collection is, it is now an offence to sell it
and you stand the risk of a heavy fine if you do.
Use only domestic or caged bird eggs.
The Endangered Species (Import and Export) Act
of 1976 states that birds' eggs cannot be
imported unless an import licence is obtained,
therefore you must check your source
very carefully before buying imported eggs.
Laws protecting wildlife universally
are complex and comprehensive and it is
wise to check with your
local Conservation Society before
choosing eggs for this craft.

Introduction

Throughout the ages the egg has been a symbol of rebirth. Coloured and decorated eggs represented the coming of spring to early civilisations. Beautifully painted or jewel-studded eggs were given to newlyweds to ensure fertility; to the young as a symbol of security and love and to the bereaved as a symbol of reincarnation of the departed soul.

With the coming of Christianity, the egg became the symbol of the resurrection of Christ and the promise of new life, and in fourth century Britain the law forbad the eating of eggs during Lent. Any eggs laid during this period were hard-boiled, coloured and given to children to play with. The oldest known decorated egg dates back to this time and was discovered in a Roman sarcophagus near Worms in Germany.

The decoration of eggs has continued as a folk art world-wide, the most beautiful and precious being the magnificent presentation eggs made for the Russian royal family by Carl Fabergé in the late nineteenth century. These eggs range from 2cm(¾in) to 37cm(14½in) high. The larger eggs are intricately designed, each containing a surprise and each worth a small fortune. It is from these fabulous creations that modern egg crafters take their inspiration. Although precious metals and stones are not used, it is a wonderful challenge to turn the simple perfect egg shape into an exquisite and lasting treasure.

When I first discovered this craft several years ago, all I had to help me was an article in a magazine. However, armed with a hacksaw blade and the largest hens' eggs I could buy, I started cutting the shells in half to make simple jewel boxes. I still have my first attempts to remind me how crude and clumsy they were, although at the time I was delighted with the results. So, don't expect perfection with your first egg. Friends started bringing me bits of broken jewellery, which I dismantled and I found cigar box hinges particularly useful for my tiny jewel box lids. Nowadays these accessories are readily available and can be bought from craft shops and specialist suppliers.

I have always felt that having to invest in expensive materials, before experimenting with a new craft, is off-putting for

Silk and cut out paper flowers decorate this delicately filigreed goose egg design which uses decoupage to its best advantage.

Three large identical prints are used. The first is made into a transfer and fixed around the egg. Then the shell is cut out around the images. A second matching transfer is made and used to line the inside of the shell. It is glued into place and any excess print is trimmed away neatly. Flowers and leaves from the left over prints are stiffened with two coats of acrylic, cut out and raised over the matching base flowers on the shell.

The egg is varnished inside and out until the raised flowers are hard. All cut edges are then trimmed with fine antique cord. I made the violets inside and over the base with nylon over gold wire. You could, of course, use delicate silk flowers.

The egg sits on a piece of dried fungus, which I found on a dead tree; this is glued to a piece of flat bark. The fungus and bark are well dried and coated with three coats of white wood glue before fixing them to the egg with strong fast-drying glue.

I occasionally find dead bees and moths in the house and keep them in a box. I thought the bee might have disintegrated but it didn't and it 'lives' again inside the egg. Small dried ivy leaves are placed here and there and given a coat of varnish to complete this garden theme.

Introduction

beginners. So I have endeavoured to keep the initial outlay to a minimum, using items and products that are easily available. The projects I have described in this book will give you confidence in handling eggs and will help you create many delightful treasures. As your confidence grows you should feel able to attempt the more exciting eggs illustrated here and you may then feel it worthwhile investing in a wider range of equipment, specialised glues, paints and glazes.

There are many different ideas and methods that can be used in egg decorating and it is impossible to describe them all. Every year somebody creates a more intricate and intriguing idea. This craft is as versatile as any you will find. It is for the artist, the pressed flower enthusiast, the miniature model maker, the engraver. I have dabbled in many other crafts over the years and spent long frustrating hours with canvas, papers and paints, trying to achieve some sort of perfection. In the end, I have always come back to the egg, where I can use the techniques and knowledge I have accumulated in these other areas.

Once you start creating your own designs it is worthwhile signing and photographing them. Who knows – if some of them survive the years undamaged they could become tomorrow's antiques! More importantly, a photographic record is a reminder of what has been created in the past. It is surprising how quickly one forgets.

The ideas contained in this book are just the tip of the iceberg. Once you have mastered the simple projects, they should inspire you to experiment and have fun creating your own designs. Both beginners and the more experienced will find endless delight in this timeless craft.

Ideas and design

Not only do eggs come in different sizes, they also vary in shape. Some are fat and almost round, others are long and pointed. This is particularly true of goose eggs. It is because the goose egg is so variable and comparatively strong, that it is a firm favourite with egg crafters everywhere. There will be times when a certain shape or size of egg will be required to carry out a project, or a particular size, shape or colour will spark off an idea. So, to some extent the egg shape will influence the design and the type of cut to be executed.

The first question a stranger to the craft will ask is "How long does it take?" I am still trying to work out the answer. It can be anything from hours to months. It is possible to work out the actual hours spent working on the shell, but there are many more hours of preparation working out the finer details. Then there's

The simple design for this egg is based on a twelfth century jewelled and banded Saracen ostrich egg. The clock mechanism can be purchased from most egg craft suppliers or clock makers and strong fast-drying glue is used to attach all the decorations to the shell.

Two round holes are cut into a plain blown ostrich shell; one at the back which is large enough to allow access into the clock works and one at the front which matches the clock face circumference exactly. The mechanism is simply glued into the shell with the strong fast-drying adhesive.

Since the clock face is flat and the egg shell is curved, the gaps are disguised with gold cord. The shell is quartered with brass bands into which individually set rhinestones are glued and the banding is edged with cord. A gold metal neck chain is fixed around the shell, above and below the brass bands. The metal leaves are applied separately.

The rear cut-out shell section is hinged on to the back of the egg on one side and a latch is fixed on the opposite side to keep it closed. A brass clock finial is mounted on top and the finished egg is glued to a brass lamp stand which sits on a black base.

The picture decorating this ostrich egg is a copy of a design which was first carefully worked out on paper, then drawn on to the shell freehand. Fairly thick acrylic paints are used on the design, then parts of the shell are cut away around the images to reveal the lamp interior.

A circle is cut into the base of the shell at this stage, to allow the light bulb through. The shell is extremely thick and the cutting takes some time. The top of the egg is cut off and a zig zag pattern is cut into the edge which is trimmed with gold cord. A circle is cut into the top of this section, to match the circle at the base of the shell and the two sections are glued together. Gold cord is attached around the two sections to hide any untidy edges.

Six coats of satin glaze are applied over the painting, then the filigreed edges and parts of the design are trimmed with thin black and gold thread. Old-gold heavy braid is used around the top and bottom of the shell.

I found the plaster lamp base in a junk shop, chipped and covered with dirty gold paint. This was stripped, repaired and repainted before attaching it to the egg. The shell is kept in place with the brass ring on the lamp holder, which is screwed down inside, just tight enough to hold the egg in place.

the leg-work involved in finding that elusive essential piece and the time waiting for glues to stick and paints to dry.

The first eggs you do will probably be copies of others you have seen. This is fine. We all copy at the beginning and in doing so gain experience and expertise, finding out by trial and error what can and can't be done. Gradually your own ideas will take over.

Although the methods of cutting may have been done many times before, it is what goes inside and outside the shell that makes it unique. How are ideas formed? My inspirations come from fairy stories, history, architecture and as in the case of the emu egg shown on page 15, the Japanese Exhibition at the Victoria and Albert Museum. Nature provides its own inspiration with a wealth of possibilities such as animals, birds, plants and marine life. Finally, of course, I find great inspiration in the fantastic Fabergé eggs. Just to make a replica of one of his beautiful works of art is an achievement in itself.

I always work out my designs on paper so that I have a visual reference. I make a note of what I aim to do, what I can make and what compromises I have to make between the ideal and the available. What matters in the end is that the whole creation should harmonise and be well proportioned, from the first cut to the final choice of stand.

So, once you have mastered the basics, be adventurous. If an idea doesn't work, at least you have found out why. Don't be afraid of working on eggs. They need firm and gentle handling. When starting I suffered a few disasters, now I make sure there is a carpet on the floor where I'm working and hope if I drop an egg it will bounce. I still get nervous when finishing an all important egg and do everything to ensure that no-one, including the cat, can get near it and accidentally knock it over!

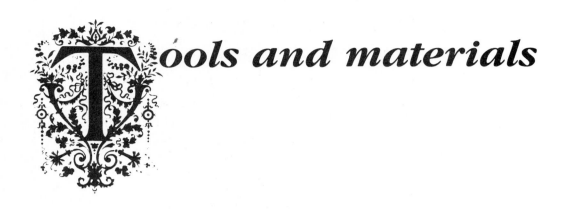ools and materials

If you are new to a craft, expensive materials can be off-putting, so I have endeavoured to keep costs down by using materials and tools that are inexpensive and readily available. As well as the types of eggs suitable for this craft, I list below the basic requirements needed to produce the eggs shown in this book.

Junior hacksaw blade or electric craft drill for cutting shells.

Face mask and goggles for protection when cutting shells.

Egg blower to remove the yolk. (For instructions on making an egg-blower, see page 21. You will need a meat baster, a clear used ball point pen and a small length of rubber or plastic tubing.)

Scissors, craft knife or scalpel.

Cocktail sticks for applying glue and mixing paints.

Egg marker or rubber bands and a soft pencil, for marking cutting lines on shells.

Egg boxes in which to lay shells while applying hinges or decorations.

White craft glue and epoxy rapid glue or strong fast-drying adhesive.

Small hinges of various sizes.

Ballentine for strengthening and decorating shells.

Plaster of Paris, or clay, to weight the egg and make it more stable.

Pots of enamel paints; watercolours or water-based paints; acrylics or acrylic based paints used for painting models; gouache; nail varnish; paint sprays. Almost any kind of paint can be used depending on the finish or effect required, even those trial pots of emulsion in your local decorators' shop. Specialised paints, including pearlised and metallic finishes, are available from egg craft suppliers.

Clear varnishes or glazes to suit the type of paint used.

Soft materials for lining.

Decorations and accessories such as braids, cord, ribbon, glitter, beads and stones, jewellery, transfers, dried flowers. Many different types of stand can be bought, or make your own using

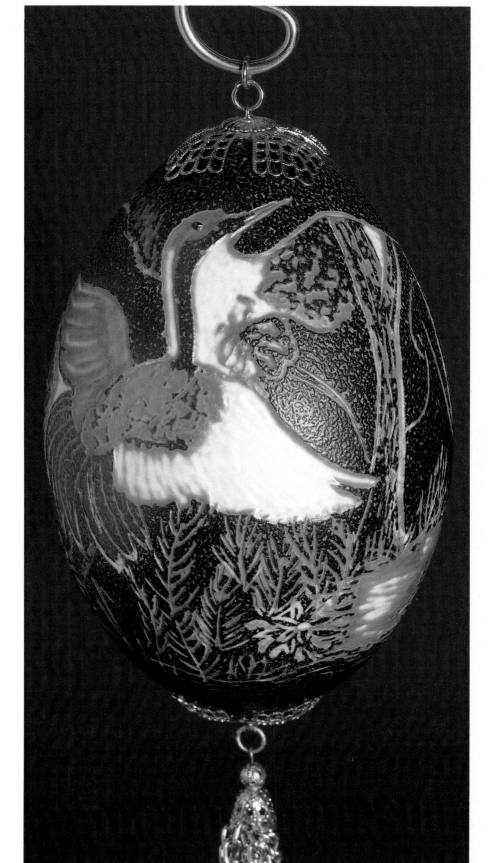

The emu shell is so unusual that I didn't want to detract from its natural beauty. These eggs are extremely difficult to come by and worthy of considerable thought before attacking them with a drill. The Aborigines in Australia engrave beautiful designs and animals on these shells, and because of the varying shades throughout the layers, this is the best decoration for the emu egg.

The design shown here is based on Japanese paintings and ivories. Drawing the picture on to the shell is a problem since ordinary paints and crayons rub off, so I use white acrylic as a guide for the basic cutting lines and the design is engraved for the most part freehand. Acrylic does not wash off so it is advisable to use it sparingly. A variety of dental burrs and craft blades are used while working through the different coloured layers of shell, from dark green to white. Once the white layer is exposed the shell is quite thin, and care has to be taken not to go through it.

Gold filigree and a tassle are attached to the bottom of the egg. A large up-eye surrounded by gold filigree is glued with strong fast-drying glue to the top. A jump ring through the up-eye enables the egg to be hooked on to a tall hanging stand.

wood or stone. A wide range of accessories is available from egg craft suppliers.

Plastic lemonade bottles with a black base serve as excellent domes for protecting favourite eggs. Remove the black base by immersing the bottle in hot water to melt the glue. The clear bottle is domed at the bottom. Then just cut the top of the bottle off, somewhere below the neck. These domes can also be used as mini cloches for plants.

Types of eggs

It is an offence to take, sell, destroy or have in one's possession any wild bird's egg. Domestic or caged bird eggs and those that can be imported can be used. If you have contacts abroad and wish to import eggs, you must obtain an import licence.

As paper or canvas supports an artist's work, so the egg shell will support your work. The type of paper or canvas the artist uses to some extent dictates the type of picture that will be produced. Similarly, certain shells lend themselves to particular ideas for a design. Size, shape and colour all determine the look of the end product. Below I have described the types of eggs I usually work with, starting with the most readily available.

Hen

I find these shells vary in strength. Any that crack during cutting or blowing are not worth trying to repair and are best discarded. White shells, which used to be more common than brown shells, are now not so easy to find. However, these are better if you want to use watercolours on them. I use hen eggs for Christmas tree decorations, cribs and Easter baskets.

Bantam

These are like hen eggs, but smaller, and in my experience the shells are much stronger.

Duck

Duck eggs vary in size. They can be almost the size of goose eggs, but they are more commonly the size of hen eggs, although the shells are quite different. They have a wonderful translucent quality about them like fine bone china. The true 'duck egg blue' shells are beautiful just varnished and with the minimum of adornments.

Quail

These small, fragile eggs are specially protected under the law although they can still be bought in some food stores. They are beige with dark brown markings. These patches of colour can vary from a few to many, covering the whole egg. The markings can be gently removed, if required, with a soap filled wire pad. Quail eggs can be bought in boxes of twelve, but since the shells are so fragile some are bound to be crushed.

Goose

These eggs can weigh anything from 140 gms (5oz) to 300 gms (11oz), the largest usually being double-yolked. The shape of the egg also varies from being fairly round, to torpedo-shaped. This is one reason why the goose egg is so versatile.

Inspiration for this egg came from some sad looking lead seagulls found at a jumble sale. I repainted the gulls with enamels using a bird book for reference.

The shell is a large oval goose egg cut in half and hinged at the back. Three young gulls are painted in watercolours on the top of the shell. The lower half of the egg and the lid interior are also painted in watercolours.

Small stones and painted pieces of plaster of Paris resembling rocks are glued into the shell and the smaller gull is positioned on top. A rock pool is made in the base of the shell by squeezing in clear glue from a tube and leaving it to set. Blanket weed, taken from a garden pond and washed thoroughly, is stranded over the rocks, and sealed with clear fast-drying craft glue.

The large gull is glued very solidly to a piece of rock to form the base. Tiny modelled eggs nestle on the front ledge of the rocks. The now heavy egg is glued with strong fast-drying adhesive to the wing supports of the base gull.

Tools and materials

Sometimes the shape will inspire a design, or maybe an idea will require a certain shape and size of egg. The one problem is that geese, as a rule, generally only lay for a few months a year. So, if you want to work on their eggs throughout the year, you have to blow them and stock them up for future use while they are available. For me, this means a lot of cooking. Omelettes and scrambled eggs can become tedious, but goose eggs make superb sponge cakes which freeze well. A culinary note here — the whites will not whip up hard for meringue recipes.

Turkey

Although similar to hen eggs, turkey eggs are slightly larger and more pointed at the 'sharp' end. They are a lovely creamy colour with irregular brown spots. A well-marked egg is attractive in its natural state. I find that several coats of varnish are all that is needed to strengthen the shell and enhance the colour, before adding any decorations or trimmings. These eggs do not appear to be very common unless you live near a turkey farm! But it is worthwhile enquiring locally before searching elsewhere.

Ostrich

The ostrich is found in South Africa and the eggs are large, approximately 38 cm (15in) in circumference. The shell is dark cream and pitted and is extremely hard to cut. In my experience the best way to cut these eggs is with a power drill.

Rhea

The rhea is a South American bird and although smaller, is related to the ostrich. The egg is greeny white in colour and is about half the size of an ostrich egg, being approximately 15 cm (6in) long.

Emu

The emu is found in Australia and its dark green egg is approximately 19 cm (7½in) in circumference. When the dark green exterior is scratched away it reveals a paler blue-green layer; beneath this the egg is white. These eggs are difficult to find and are very expensive. They are not the sort to practice on!

A goose egg shell base makes a lovely mount for this beautiful rose painted on silk. This print started life as a padded picture in a hideous gold plastic frame. These types of framed silk are fairly common and come in various sizes and scenes.

Remove the picture from its frame and separate the silk from the padding. Coat the egg shell with a thin coat of white craft glue. Place the print on to the shell and smooth out any air bubbles or creases.

The picture is framed with a row of gold strung beads set between two rows of gold cord. A deep looped braid is added beneath the three top rows.

# Techniques

Preparation and cleaning

Before starting, and if the fresh egg is dirty, wash it using a little detergent. Some goose and duck eggs are not only dirty, but stained, and a good scrub with a soap-filled wire wool pad should do the trick. Unfortunately some stains refuse to be moved and these eggs will have to be painted. Some coloured markings can also be removed by gently scrubbing the egg with the wire pad.

Blowing the Egg

In most cases the egg contents need to be removed before starting work on the egg. This is called 'blowing' the egg. It is always wise to blow your eggs if you are planning to store them for future use. However, with smaller eggs, such as hen, duck and

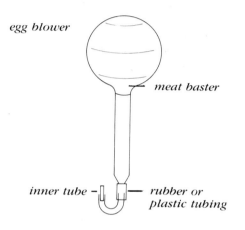

egg blower

meat baster

inner tube — *rubber or plastic tubing*

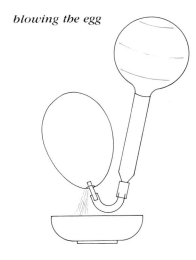

blowing the egg

quail, the shells are easier to cut if they are not blown, and if you are planning to use them straightaway it is better to use unblown eggs. Since the shells are quite fragile, the contents will lend some support whilst the egg is held in a firm grip.

Fresh goose eggs will keep for about six weeks in the refrigerator but if you want to eat duck eggs use them as fresh as possible and cook them well. Always remove eggs you are going to blow from the refrigerator several hours beforehand and allow them to warm to room temperature. The contents are then more liquid and run out more easily.

The traditional way to blow an egg is to make a hole at each end. I either use a drill, or a hole can be made by tapping a metal meat skewer through the shell. The skewer will make the correct size opening, but inevitably the edges will be a little ragged and chipped. With the skewer, or a long needle, break up the egg contents inside the shell. With a dish at the ready, blow through the hole at one end of the egg and the contents should flow out through the other end. This is hard work unless the holes are fairly large, but these can be covered by beads or braids when decorating the egg later. With a little trouble it is possible to make a reasonably efficient 'egg blower'.

An ordinary meat baster can be used, as long as it has a fine enough end. This looks like a large syringe and can be bought from hardware or kitchen stores. If the end of the baster is too large, then a little improvisation is required. You will need a clear, used ballpoint pen, with its inner tube empty of ink and a 2.5cm(1in) length of rubber or plastic tubing.

Remove the ink tube from the outer case of the pen and cut off approximately 5cm(2in) from the cleanest part, discarding the rest. Thoroughly wash this part and the outer casing. Heat the casing by holding one end of it very carefully over a flame until it is soft enough to curve round. Don't make the curve too sharp or the air passage inside will close up. Join this to the meat baster with the length of tubing. Insert the 5cm(2in) section of ink tube into the curved end of the casing, leaving about 2.5cm(1in) exposed. You now have an egg blower that will last forever if it is washed and dried well after each use.

With a dish ready to catch the egg contents, make a hole at one end of the egg shell only. With the hole held over the dish, insert the blower and push air into the egg by squeezing the bulb. Don't release the bulb until you have removed the tube from the egg, or you will fill the blower with the egg contents instead of air! Insert the blower into the egg again and keep repeating this process, as the air forces first the white and then the yolk to run out into the dish. When the shell is quite empty, wash it out by filling the blower with hot soapy water and squeezing it back into the shell. Shake the shell well and empty as before. Leave to drain out and dry.

Techniques

Cutting

There are many different ways of cutting egg shells and the more basic and simple cuts are illustrated in this section. Variations in the basic cuts can be seen by looking at the designs throughout the book. It might seem that the most complicated cuts belong to the 'Photograph Album' egg, (see page 88) and 'Sleeping Beauty', (see page 93), but their basic cuts are illustrated in this section. They have been adapted and varied slightly to suit the design, so this is all discussed under each project heading.

Simple straight cuts can be used on jewel boxes, bells, flowers and eggs that contain scenes or some hidden surprise; more complicated cutting can be used to enhance the colours or design of a particular egg. Unless cut edges are perfect, these always have to be covered by braid or cord, so don't worry too much about ragged edges!

Simple but effective, this tiny quail egg provides its own decorations with its random shell markings.

After the lid is cut off, several coats of varnish are applied to both top and bottom sections to strengthen the shell. The inside is coated with clear fast-drying glue and ballentine is applied.

The edges are trimmed with cord and a tiny pearl crowns the lid. The handles are made using a pair of ear wires set into tiny gold findings. The egg sits on a solid brass stand.

cutting line

rubber band

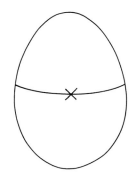

*x for matching two halves
after cutting*

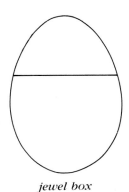

jewel box

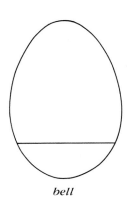

bell

The easiest way to cut the shell is to use an electric craft drill with a circular blade and if you intend to do a lot of cutting, then it is worthwhile investing in one. They come in various sizes and prices vary accordingly. My original little drill, which runs off a transformer or car battery, has proved perfectly adequate for many years. I also have an old portable dentist's drill. Now more sophisticated cutters are available including the air drill. There are a variety of blades and bits which can be used with these drills, but the cheapest and most useful is the carborundum disc. This comes in various sizes. For the more complicated cuts and filigrees, this piece of equipment is essential.

For the beginner, the humble junior hacksaw blade works just as well on simple, straight cuts, but a drill is quicker, more versatile and is better for cutting smooth, even curves.

If you are buying smaller eggs, such as hen, duck and quail eggs, and you are cutting them within a few days, it is easier to cut them if they are not blown. Since the shells are quite fragile the contents will lend some support whilst the egg is held in a firm grip. If you are storing them, then they need to be blown.

Straight cuts

I always mark the cutting line, or design, on the shell with a soft pencil before beginning to cut. Egg markers are available from egg craft suppliers, but I find a thick rubber band gives as good a guideline for a straight cut. Using a band that will fit snugly around the shell, place it either horizontally or vertically, according to your design. Check that it is quite straight and mark out the cutting line with the pencil. Remove the band.

If the cut is around the 'waist' of the shell, mark a cross on the pencil line, since once the shell is cut it is difficult to match up the two halves exactly without a guide. This cross can also mark where the hinge will be sited.

If you are going to cut the shell using an electric craft tool, it is essential to wear goggles or spectacles to protect your eyes from flying chips. It is even more essential to wear a mask of some sort. Goose and larger egg shells create a lot of fine dust, which in large quantities can affect the lungs. If the shell is not too fragile, it is possible to score the design first, tracing around the lines with a small groove. This is done by exerting a gentle pressure as the circular or hacksaw blade cuts into the shell. However, if the egg is fragile, the blade will cut right through both shell and membrane.

Use your thumb as a support if you are using the hacksaw blade, (a drill just needs a steady hand and eye). Score evenly round and round the shell until the membrane is reached. The blade may be inclined to skid on a smooth shell at first, but once a slight groove is made it is just a matter of patience and perseverance. Don't be afraid to hold the shell firmly — they don't crush that

Techniques

easily when whole. Keep the groove smooth and avoid penetrating the shell in one area if using the hacksaw, before moving on to the next section. I find the deeper you score round the shell before actually cutting through the membrane, the better.

Once the membrane is penetrated things start to get a little messy if the egg has not been blown, so have a bowl and damp cloth ready to wipe your hands. After cutting, wash and dry the shell, ensuring all the egg white has been removed. Leave the membrane inside the shell intact as this provides added strength. If parts have come away during washing, smooth them back into place before drying.

If shells are cut for future use they must be taped back together carefully, since they are inclined to warp over a long period and then the separate parts do not match up exactly.

Curved and angled cuts

Gentle curves and angles add to the beauty of the smooth egg shape. Large curves, such as the curved lid, or even large doors, can be marked on to the shell using an elastic band. But make sure the band is snug enough to fit the shell while the line is pencilled in.

Cuts like the sunray can also be drawn on to the egg shell using the rubber band as a marker. If you are planning to attempt this

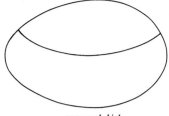

curved lid

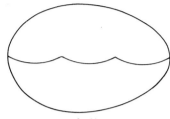

shell

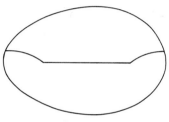

Prussian

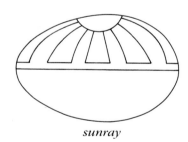

sunray

The sunray cut described opposite is used to make this lovely goose egg design; a rose coloured taffeta lining sets off the silver enamelled exterior beautifully.

The shell is hinged at the back and all cut edges are trimmed with matching silver braid. Inside edges are also trimmed with braid to give a neat finish.

The lid is topped with an old gunmetal grey earring and the egg is set on a three-legged reversible stand.

24

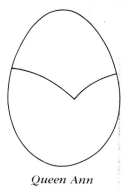

Queen Ann

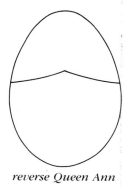

reverse Queen Ann

cut, use a goose egg. I have found that the stronger the shell the better when creating the sunray egg. Draw the horizontal line so that the shell is cut in half. Draw another line about 0.5cm(¼in) above. Using a round or oval template, draw the sun, either in the centre of the lid, or towards the farther end of the shell. Using the rubber band and a good eye, draw in the sun's rays from the sun circle to the top horizontal line. Mark the sections to be cut out clearly so you don't make a mistake and cut through the rays! Shells cut in this way are very fragile until painted and strengthened with decorations.

If my idea for a design involves smaller curves, circles or angles, I make a paper template. With a soft pencil I transfer the design on to the egg shell. In the case of the scalloped cut I use the edge of a coin. On some of the eggs illustrated in this book I have painted the design or picture freehand, straight on to the shell. Once the pencil markings or painted pictures have been drawn on to the shell, start to cut out the design.

Larger curves can be created with the hacksaw, but I find you end up with a series of short straight lines and a ragged appearance. Don't be put off, because rough edges can be hidden by colourful neat braids and trims.

Smaller curves, circles and angles are better made with the craft drill. This ensures a smooth, even cut. The sunray cut and

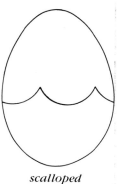

scalloped

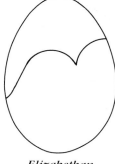

Elizabethan

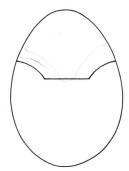

Prussian cap

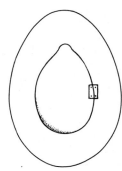

mosque

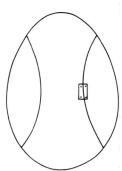

opposite side doors

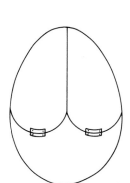

petal

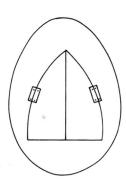

church door

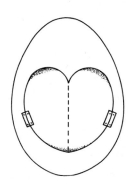

one or two door heart

the filigree cuts illustrated throughout the book are only possible with a drill. These are more complicated and require a measure of dexterity and skill. This will only come with practice, so try out your skills on the more simple eggs first. Follow the lines of the design holding the egg firmly. Don't forget to wear your mask and goggles as protection against flying dust and particles!

Small doors and lids can be cut out with the electric drill and attached to the shell with tiny hinges. Simple or intricate designs can be carved out revealing beautiful interiors. Once the cutting technique is mastered, the simple egg can be turned into a work of art, or a lasting treasure.

Cutting a drawer

Once you have mastered cutting the shell, you can be really adventurous and amaze your friends with an egg containing a working drawer. It is not too difficult, but rather fiddly.

A goose egg is perfect for this type of design. For the actual drawer you will need the inside section of a small matchbox. Make sure this will fit into your shell. The section of shell to be cut for the front of the drawer must be slightly larger, on all four sides, than the end of the box.

Cut the shell as for an upright jewel box, but cut a little higher than the waist of the egg, otherwise the drawer will be too low; or cut a door in the top half of the shell as illustrated on the page opposite. Measure and mark out the drawer front on to the shell with a pencil, according to the size of the matchbox front. Make sure the top of the drawer is at least 1 cm (½in) below the rim.

Cut out the drawer with great care. A sharp pointed tomato knife will be easier than the hacksaw blade for the short sides, but this is one of those times when an electric craft drill is vastly superior.

Paint the matchbox inside and out with enamel, to match the colour and design of the egg. Paint the shell drawer front, and do keep this tiny piece safe from breakage until required.

To make the drawer support, cut two cocktail sticks to fit inside the shell in the form of a 'V' from front to back, just below the drawer opening. Glue in position, using epoxy rapid adhesive.

Glue the drawer front to the matchbox front with strong rapid-setting glue, allowing the glue to fill the space between the matchbox front and the slight curve of the shell. If the gap is an obvious one then it can be hidden with a strip of cord or narrow braid. Use a narrow cord as trimming around the edge of the drawer front. A suitable jewel, glued to the centre of the drawer, will act as a handle.

Now cut a piece of stiff card, the same width and slightly longer than the back of the matchbox. This is going to stop the drawer from being pulled right out. Slide the drawer into the egg a little, and glue the card on to the back.

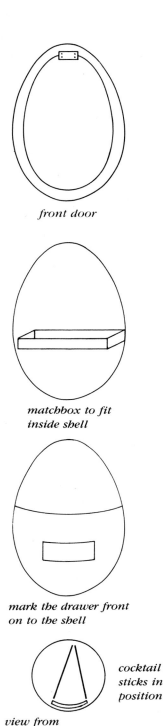

front door

matchbox to fit inside shell

mark the drawer front on to the shell

cocktail sticks in position

view from above

stiff card

glue the drawer front to the matchbox front

This goose egg has a drawer and a door opening. After cutting, the egg is enamelled dark green. It is lined with satin and all edges are trimmed with gold braid. Gold metal leaves decorate the four corners of the drawer opening.

The tiny Victorian style brass drawer knob is of the type used by miniature furniture makers. The finished egg is glued on to a tall, elegant stand which complements the design.

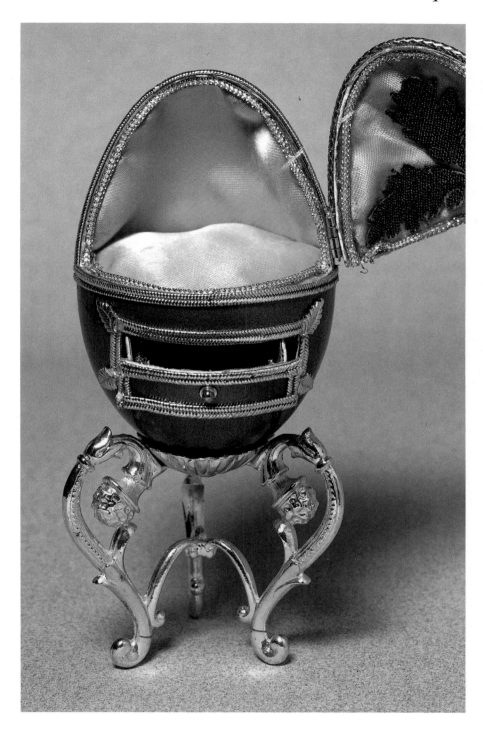

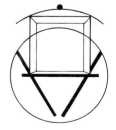

view from above showing cocktail stick runners and drawer stop

To hide the drawer mechanics, a platform is needed above the drawer in the lower half of the egg. Measure the circumference inside the shell, just below the rim of the bottom shell and cut a disc from stiff card to fit. Use a compass to draw the circle. Cover the disc with soft material which should harmonise with the design and colours of the egg.

Put a line of craft glue around the shell interior and ease the disc into position. Since the egg opening is likely to be smaller

Three cuts are used on the heavily jewelled and braided goose egg shown on these pages.

The front section has a window set into it. This is achieved by cutting out an oval of shell, turning it round back to front, and gluing it back into the space to form a dish. A similar shaped piece of clear plastic is used to cover it. Using acrylics, a tree is painted on to the inside of the plastic dome to create a three dimensional effect.

The front and sides are hinged and lift up to reveal a tiny duck on a mirror pond, surrounded by miniature dried grasses and flowers. The side openings enable the duck pond to be viewed from different angles. The country scene is painted on the inside of the shell with acrylics and followed on to the side panels. Plaster of Paris is used to weight the egg and supports the little pond.

The shell exterior is trimmed with an assortment of braids and rhinestones. A pair of gold metal leaves form a handle for the front opening, and gold tassels are used on the side panels. A gold and crystal finial tops the egg, which is supported by an elaborate gold stand set on marble.

than the disc, you will have to gently bend the card a little to get it in. Open the drawer and insert a pair of tweezers to support the platform from underneath and hold in place until the adhesive has set enough to stop it slipping down. Edge the join, where the platform meets the shell, with cord or fine braid.

The lid can be lined, or painted, then hinged in place. Add any exterior decorations. These techniques are all described on the following pages.

Cutting a window

This is not as hard as it looks and is achieved by cutting and reversing a piece of shell, and covering it with a piece of curved clear plastic to follow the curve of the shell.

I used to buy any clear plastic eggs I could find during the Easter period for my windows. It is only recently I have discovered that lemonade bottles work just as well. They can also easily be cut with scissors, whereas some of the egg shaped covers on Easter eggs were extremely hard and had to be cut with a steel blade on the electric drill.

Assuming you wish to insert a window in the lid of a horizontal cut egg, or in a large door, as in the illustrations on pages 28 and 89, first you have to do the basic cut. Decide upon the size of the window, bearing in mind that you have to leave sufficient shell around the edge of the window, as this area will be extremely fragile and must be no less than 1cm(½in). Draw an oval on to the shell, once you have decided upon the position of the window. It is better to use a template, or you can draw it freehand if you feel confident enough. Cut out the shell window using the electric drill. Remember that the remaining shell will be very fragile, so handle it carefully.

Using the cut out oval of shell, place it over the curved area near the neck of the lemonade bottle, seeking out a part that matches as near as possible the convex shape of the shell. Draw around the outside of the shell with a marker pen, then cut out the piece of plastic.

Reverse the piece of shell and set it into the original section of shell from which the oval was cut, using either thinly applied fast epoxy, or a strong white craft glue. Carefully clean away any surplus adhesive.

The inside of your little showcase can now be fitted with a tiny dried flower arrangement, bread dough flowers or you could paint a miniature picture. Paint the outer border and inside to match the rest of the egg design. Glue the plastic dome over the reversed shell and cover up the joins with cord or tiny braid.

Raising designs before painting

If you are planning to paint a picture on to your shell, gesso can be used to raise the whole image, or part of the picture, before

The shell of this goose egg is cut into three parts – the front, back and base. It is hinged, the two main areas folding down to reveal a beautiful scene inside. A goldfinch and a kingfisher decorate the closed egg. Gesso is used to raise the bodies and wings of the birds so they can be painted over and disguised.

The two birds and surrounding plants are drawn on to the shell and lightly painted in with watercolours as a guide for applying the gesso. When the gesso is dry, the painting is completed and parts of the shell cut out with a craft drill. The egg is then hinged together and the gesso applied to the hinges to disguise them.

The base shell is painted and then the whole egg is varnished with a combination of painted foliage and pressed flowers, and then covered with a layer of ballentine. A swan sits in the centre on a plaster of Paris lake surrounded by dried grasses.

The wooden plinth is painted. The base of this design contains a bird song mechanism. This is glued into a velvet covered plastic pot.

applying any colours. It takes a bit of careful planning at the design stage, but the finished effect is worth it. This technique was used for the kingfisher and goldfinch birdsong egg shown on the previous page, raising the body and parts of the wings slightly away from the shell.

Before applying the gesso, sand down the shell as described in the following section. Gesso is a plaster and can be found in most art shops. It is a powder which is mixed with water to a creamy consistency before application. I use a glue syringe to apply the gesso, but a fine paint brush could be used as effectively.

Gesso can be used wherever you want to raise a design before painting. It should be applied in layers, allowing each to dry before adding the next, until the required height is achieved. Keep any left over gesso in a pot covered with a damp cloth and it can be used for several days.

Painting and colouring

Beautiful effects can be achieved by painting pictures straight on to a blown egg. These can be cut out or filigreed; an example of the painting technique is shown opposite. In all other cases the paint is applied *after* cutting, or before decorating the shells in the case of uncut designs, like the Christmas tree baubles shown at the top of page 73. There are many types of paints that can be used and it is fun to experiment with the huge range of colours

This was one of the first goose eggs that I worked on. It was a large double-yolked one and had I realised these were fairly rare, I might have saved the shell for something more adventurous. However, I was pleased with my first attempt with watercolours.

The varnish I used in those days altered the colours somewhat, as the painting was more yellow than it now appears. These days I only use colourless varnishes. Although my fixing of hinges and braids has improved over the years, this still remains one of my favourite eggs.

An oval wooden frame complements the simple egg shape and half a goose egg makes a change from paper or canvas on which to paint your masterpiece. This is a picture of Beachy Head in Sussex painted in acrylics.

After the painting is finished and given a coat of matt varnish, a thin layer of plaster is spread over the back of the shell to add strength. If your frame contains glass, remove the glass and cover the backing card with velvet.

Strong fast-drying glue is applied to the inside rim of the shell fairly thickly, so that it runs down when the shell is laid flat on the velvet. Lay the frame flat and as soon as the glue is applied to the shell, place it in exactly the right position – if it has to be moved around too much, unsightly patches of glue will mark the velvet.

Once the shell is firmly fixed, trim around with cord or braid, where the shell meets the velvet.

and tones. If the egg is intended for a special occasion such as Christmas or an anniversary, choose an appropriate colour.

Not all shells, especially the goose egg shell, are perfectly smooth. They often have a few raised spots and rough areas. Using a medium grain sandpaper, smooth away those areas. Finish with a fine grain paper over the entire shell to give a smooth base for the paint-work. This applies to any project you attempt. Wipe away any dust with a damp cloth before painting. Don't paint over the hinge mark (x), if you have marked one. It is a good idea to hold the shell at this part with finger and thumb whilst applying the paint.

Be sure the shells are in a dust-free environment whatever type of paint you use. Don't be tempted to set the shell aside and then start cutting another shell in the same room; it would spell disaster. If the painted surface is not perfect, no matter what else you do, the end product will never look professional.

33

Techniques

Although personally I hate doing the same egg twice, in the case of the Christmas tree eggs shown on page 73, the uncut shells can be mass-produced by painting them all the same colour. I have devised a simple and efficient way of doing this by hammering a row of long nails into a flat piece of wood. Place a shell on each nail using the blow hole, before applying the several coats of paint. If you find the shell is loose on the nail and turns round when you are trying to use long even brush strokes, a little clay to block the hole between the shell and the nail should solve the problem.

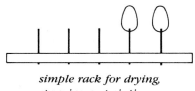

simple rack for drying, spraying or painting blown uncut shells

Specialised paints with metallic or pearlised finishes are available from egg craft suppliers. These can be applied direct to the shell, although always remember to read the manufacturers' instructions. As well as these, non-specialised paints can be used. I have experimented with many different types, but have found that the following achieve excellent results.

Water-based paints

In my experience, as egg shells are slightly greasy, if using gouache, watercolours, or any water-based paint, it is better to lay a base coat of white acrylic over the shell before applying any colours. Just paint your design or picture straight on to this layer of paint, as you would on paper or canvas.

Acrylics

The strength and durability of acrylics make them ideal for this craft. They do not darken with time, although there is a slight deepening of tone as the paint dries. This has to be allowed for if you are painting a matching colour over a layer of paint that has already hardened. Acrylics can be used undiluted, or diluted with water. Lay a base coat of white paint on to your shell if you are intending to use diluted colours.

Enamels

Enamels can be painted straight on to the shell. Several coats give a lustrous finish reminiscent of the beautiful Fabergé eggs; five or six coats are usually enough. The little pots of enamel paint sold to model makers are ideal, but do make sure they are fresh and not old stock, or the finish will not be so smooth and brilliant. Let the paint dry well between coats.

Wonderful marbling effects can be achieved by using two or three different coloured enamel paints. I have used this as a quick and simple form of decoration on many small eggs and in a variety of colours. I have in the past used this method on larger goose eggs, but somehow it never looked quite right, so now I restrict its use to smaller shells.

Choose one dominant colour and paint the shell in the normal way. Whilst still wet, drip on small blobs of a second colour using

This goose egg is carefully
measured and marked before
cutting the shell with an electric
craft tool.

Pink acrylics decorate the shell
and the interior is coated with
ballentine. The top of the shell is
covered with mother-of-pearl
flakes and then varnished. Rows of
pearls and braid adorn the edges.
The pearl finial is surrounded by
four pearl leaves.

A thin layer of plaster of Paris in
the bottom of the shell supports a
card disc which is covered with
dried pondweed and a single coat
of varnish. The little goose girl
model is brightened up with two
coats of a special porcelain
finished varnish. The finished egg
sits on a tall elegant stand on an
onyx base.

a cocktail stick dipped into the paint pot. The colours will run and blend. By running the tip of the cocktail stick horizontally through the running spots of paint, veins of colour are produced. If you want to use a third colour, repeat this process. Leave the shell to dry. As you watch, the colours will run creating wonderful patterns. Unfortunately you can't stop the process when you see one you like! Try different combinations of colours. White is a good base, with dark green dripped on followed by a little black; the finished effect resembles green marble. Red, or a dark green base with a little white and black, is effective; also browns and yellows. It's fun experimenting.

Spray paints

Excellent results can be achieved by using paint sprays. I usually carry out my spraying outside on a good wind-free day in the summer, thus minimizing the risk of breathing in the spray, or my kitchen developing unwanted spots of colour! I then store the shells for decoration at a later date. If you have a garage or an outbuilding you could do it there, but do wear a mask. Aerosol paint, like hair lacquer, hangs in the air for a long time in a confined space even though you can't see it, and breathing it in should be avoided.

If you have to paint your eggs indoors, it must be done in a box to protect your room. Cover a table with newspaper and place a large cardboard box on top, with the opening facing you. Fill a small yoghurt carton, or similar, with clay. Insert a thin stick, or knitting needle, into the clay and place the shell on to it using the blow hole. Make sure the needle is long enough to ensure that the shell is clear of the carton.

Read the instructions on the spray can and make sure there is enough distance between the spray and the egg shell. Place the shell well back in the box and spray lightly. Turn the carton round between each burst of paint so that the shell is completely covered with paint. Check the area underneath the shell as it always seems to miss the paint! When the paint has dried, remove the shell and repeat the process with the next shell.

The simple rack, mentioned at the beginning of the painting section, also comes in useful if you want to spray a lot of shells the same colour. Place a shell on each nail, take the rack of shells into the garden and spray. Do check which way the breeze is blowing even if it seems to be a calm day or you and your plants could end up brightly coloured!

Nail varnish

Nail varnish can produce some exciting results and it comes in a lovely variety of jewel colours these days. It is a bit tricky when applied over large areas because it dries so quickly. The first two or three coats will look very uneven, but don't panic! Just keep

The eggs for these flowers came from an extremely obliging Aylesbury duck called Waddle, who laid identically sized eggs consistently. It was the size and shape of her eggs that inspired the tulips. They were entirely my own invention as I had never seen tulips created from egg shells before; I have since then, but not made in the same way. Sadly Waddle is no more, but I have kept enough of her eggs, which are blown and stored, ready for future use.

To make one tulip, two identically shaped shells are each marked into three petals, with the blow holes at the base. The first shell forms the inner petals and is only cut from about halfway down the shell, at the sides of each petal. The second shell is cut into three separate petals.

Study pictures of real tulips so that the colours and markings are as authentic as possible. Paint all the petals inside and out with acrylics, then apply two or three coats of matt or gloss varnish.

Take three flower wires and bind the ends together with a piece of yellow stocking. Surround this with black stamens tied in place with cotton. Using green florists' tape, wrap the wire from top to bottom binding the stamens firmly. Thread this 'stem' through the blow hole at the base of the shell and glue with strong fast-drying adhesive.

Glue the individual exterior petals on to the base petals separately with the adhesive by placing a little glue inside the base of each petal. Fix to the inner shell near the stem and hold there, slightly away from the inner shell until firmly attached. When the other two petals are in position, bind florists' tape around the stem until a suitable thickness is achieved.

These tulips were prize-winners at an Egg Crafters' Guild competition.

adding more layers, allowing each one to dry well. You may well use a whole bottle before you are satisfied with the result.

Dyeing

If the idea of painting the egg shell does not appeal to you, dyeing is a simple and effective way of colouring the whole egg. Onion skins, dark-coloured fruit such as elderberries or blackberries, and even food dyes can be used.

Put the blown egg shell, or shells, into a pan of boiling water, making sure they are well-covered. If you are using vegetables or fruit, add these to the pan with the shells, plus a spoonful of vinegar to fix the dye. If you are using food dye, just add a few drops to the boiling water. Boil the shells for approximately twenty minutes, making sure that they are completely immersed. If the shells keep popping up above the water level, prod them down with a wooden spoon. This ensures a beautiful, even all-over colour. Remove the shells from the water and allow them to cool and dry.

Varnishing

I usually add several coats of varnish to my painted designs. I find that this not only adds lustre and shine, it also strengthens the fragile shells. Always read the manufacturers' instructions before applying your varnish and make sure it is compatible with your base paint. For example, clear enamel varnish should be used with enamel paints. Each coat should be dry before the next coat is applied. Before varnishing over a watercolour design, spray the shell with a fixative, (available from art shops).

Varnish can also be applied to other forms of decoration after items have been fixed on to the shell. This is covered in the section on 'Decorations and accessories', (see page 44).

Strengthening the shell

Ballentine is wonderful for strengthening shells and is highly decorative as it gives a pretty three dimensional finish. It looks very much like glitter, but is comprised of tiny glass balls. I apply it to the insides and outsides of some of my designs both to toughen and decorate the shells. Cover the areas you want to strengthen with adhesive, then sprinkle the ballentine quite thickly over the glue and tap the shell gently to shake off the excess.

Applying a hinge

Having cut and painted the shell, if you are making a simple jewel box or scene, the next stage is applying the hinge. In some of the more complicated designs hinges are applied either at an earlier stage before painting, in cases where you have to match up continuous designs on the lid and base of the egg, or at a later stage, as with the Wedding Album, (see page 88) and the Sleeping Beauty, (see page 93). Both of the projects are explained in detail and the technique is as described in this section. Since the fixing of the hinge is the most tricky part of egg decorating, it would not be a bad idea to practise on one or two cheap undecorated shells before you attempt your masterpiece.

The choice of hinge is important. Too small and the lid will move from side to side. Too large and it will look cumbersome and stand away from the shell at the sides. A 1 cm (½in) brass

A simple hinged goose egg provides the perfect setting for this delightful scene.

A mother and baby seal rest on their plaster of Paris rocks inside the shell. The lid carries a watercolour painting of a seal on the outside and the inside is painted to represent sea and sky. White sand sprinkled on to glue, sea-shells and dried pondweed surround the seals and the edges of the shell are also trimmed with dried pondweed. I don't like using braids on 'nature' eggs and always keep the design as natural as possible.

The stand is a simple piece of flat bark decorated with a few seashells.

hinge should be easy to come by and is suitable for most large eggs. Try the hinge and if it is stiff, work it back and forth with your fingers until it loosens up. Use a little oil if necessary. Ideally it should hold in any position without undue force.

With a pair of pliers, bend the sides a little so that its shape is nearer that of the curve of the shell. It won't be exact since you can't bend the hinge post, but it will look better. Filing off the corners of the hinge is also an improvement, but if it is to be completely covered by braid, it is not essential. The underside of

Originally the goose egg shown on these two pages was intended to be just a painted scene of swans around an uncut shell. Only after completing the painting did I decide to cut away some of the design. I then applied ballentine to the swans to give a pretty, three dimensional effect.

I raised the branches and swans with gesso to give them added strength and repainted them, before cutting away parts of the shell around the design.

It wasn't until a much later date that, thinking the inside looked rather bleak when viewed through the cut out parts, I decided to make a door and set a scene inside. I carefully cut out the door around the swan and set a hinge on the lower right hand side, where the shell was not cut away.

The interior is painted and decorated with tiny flowers and dried grasses. The pond is one of several pieces of glass found on the beach and smoothed by the sea. A repainted lead swan and her cygnets float on the pond. All the cut edges are finished with gold thread and the egg is set on a fine gold stand.

the hinge can also be roughened with coarse sandpaper to aid adherence.

Set aside the prepared hinge. Assemble an egg box in which to lay the egg, some sticky tape, cocktail sticks and super epoxy rapid glue.

If you have cut the egg around the 'waist' of the shell, you will already have marked a cross indicating where the hinge will be sited. If you have not marked a cross, choose your hinge area. Tape the two parts of the shell together on either side of the hinge area, lining the cross up on the two halves if it is marked. Lay the taped sections carefully in the egg box making sure they will remain steady while the hinge is setting. If the sections move at all, the glue and the hinge will slide.

Mix the glue on a piece of card, or in a foil container or old lid. It is inevitable that you will mix more than you require since

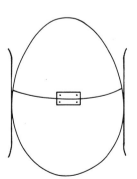

tape the two parts of the shell together

40

only the tiniest amount is needed. It is most important that you read the manufacturers' instructions before applying the glue to the hinge.

The worst thing that can happen during this process is that glue gets on to the hinge post. If it does and it is allowed to set hard, the egg will not open; so work carefully and neatly and don't overdo the glue.

Use your fingers, or a pair of tweezers, to hold the hinge. With a cocktail stick, smear a thin layer of glue on to the shell, on the hinge area. Do not go too near the edges of the shell and cover an area within the size limit of the hinge. Cover the underside of the hinge with a thin layer of glue, keeping it well away from the hinge post.

Lowering the hinge on to the shell, place it as near as possible in the correct position, with the hinge post in line with the cut shell. The more you move the hinge around once on the egg, the more chance there is of glue seeping on to the hinge post, so try to place the hinge accurately.

When satisfied, lightly press down both sides of the hinge, as tight to the shell as it will go. Check again that the hinge post is in line with the cut. If glue seeps out of the pin holes and edges of the hinge, dip your fingers in water to stop them sticking to the hinge whilst pressing it in place.

Although the glue should be set in five minutes, it will not be hard. To remove any excess that has oozed out, dip a craft knife or razor blade in water and very carefully cut through the glue at the edge of the hinge and lift it away. Keep the blade wet and remove any unwanted glue.

After a further ten minutes or so, remove the sticky tape and very carefully open the two sections. If the hinge works freely replace the tapes, ensuring the two sections are exactly together and leave the shell, supported hinge uppermost, for several hours, or overnight, to harden fully. After an hour or so just check once again that the hinge works.

If the worst has happened at either checking stage and the egg won't open with ease, it probably means that glue has seeped on to the hinge post. There is still a chance to rescue it!

If the two sections open a little, gently open and close them a fraction at a time, which will hopefully break up a small amount of glue. Do not force things or the shell will start to crack around the hinge. If the shell will open wide enough to insert a thin craft knife blade, then saw the blade across the inside of the hinge post in the hope of cutting through any excess glue.

If the absolute disaster occurs and the shell won't open at all, with a little luck the hinge can be removed altogether by immersing it in very hot, almost boiling water. This is a last resort and it does not always work. If it doesn't, I'm afraid it's back to the drawing board and on to the next egg!

A simple straight cut around the 'waist' of a goose egg can be used to create an unusual scene like the one illustrated here.

I made the toadstools and mushrooms from surplus bread dough (one mixture makes an awful lot of flowers!). As always I referred to a book on fungi to ensure the correct shape and colours.

The egg is decorated with a watercolour woodland scene. Where the painting covers the entire egg, the shell must be hinged first. The hinge is then covered with gesso to blend in with the painting.

The frog and leaf stand completes the design. As the original bright gold of the stand was not in keeping with the rest of the design it has been painted over with dark brown enamel. The gold highlights are created by wiping away some of the enamel with tissues while the paint is still wet.

Decorations and accessories

Having prepared and painted the egg, the next step is to embark on the fun part of decorating the shell; there are many exciting decorative possibilities. If the egg is intended for a special occasion such as Christmas, gold, silver or other wedding anniversary, choose appropriate colours and decorations. Christmas things need to sparkle, so you can go a bit over the top with the glitter and other bright additions to your shells. Silver and gold spray paints, along with holly, glitter and other decorations, are often only to be found in the few weeks before and after Christmas. So if you want to start making Christmas eggs in October, or earlier, you must remember to buy these things the year before!

If I want to apply initials or dates to one of my designs, I always resort to the transfer variety of lettering, as my calligraphy is not up to the professional standard I strive for! If you don't consider yourself a competent artist, colourful waterslide transfers are a good idea. Even if you can paint, there are some pretty transfers available and they are a quick and easy way to cover the shell.

Beautiful effects can be created with decoupage, using pretty wrapping paper or greetings cards, and several identical flower prints can be used to make a raised three dimensional flower arrangement; or you can use pressed flowers or tiny bread dough blooms.

Bought or made models can add interest and another dimension to the egg shape and lovely scenes can be created inside the shell with an assortment of dried grasses, miniatures and a little imagination.

Braids, jewels, sequins, lace, velvet and a variety of fabrics can all be applied to the painted egg. I find almost anything can be added, as long as it complements the design as a whole. I have tried to cover all the decorations in this section, but I am sure there are many more ideas and areas to be explored. It is up to you to experiment with the information I have given you here.

Fabrics and edgings

For those of you who enjoy working with fabrics, some quite stunning effects can be achieved fairly simply by covering the shell with fabric and a beautiful range of braids, cords, ribbons and lace can be bought from almost any department store.

Choose thin fabrics that will stretch, so that the material will mould to the shape of the curves of the egg. Some velvets, or mesh-type materials, are ideal. If the fabric is too thick any folds or gathers that form will be lumpy and unsightly.

It is impossible to cover a whole egg with a single piece of material. Once I have blown the egg, I cut it in half and work on each section; or on more complicated designs, I apply the material to each section separately.

This beautifully decorated goose egg is pure Fabergé and is based on his fabulous Caucacus egg. Each of the four doors opens to reveal a photograph, and these are set into the shell in exactly the same way as shown in the project for the photograph album egg (see page 88). All the decorations are fixed on to the egg with strong fast-drying glue.

A fairly round goose shell is required; using a template mark out four doors equidistant around the egg. Number them and number each opening before assembling — however careful the cutting, one door will not exactly match another opening.

The shell is painted with special white/gold paint; the insides of each door are painted gold and trimmed with gold thread. The doors are fixed on to the shell with small but firm ¼" hinges and edged with rhinestones and gold thread, and openings are trimmed with gold braid, pearls and gold thread.

Pairs of gold coloured filigrees form arches above and below the door openings, and a crystal and gold crown completes the design. The egg is glued to a gold dolphin stand.

A simple velvet and lace covered goose egg makes a lovely container for rings. Inside is a velvet covered foam base with a slit along it to hold one or two rings.

I rarely cover a whole shell with material as I feel this detracts from the beauty of using real eggs but it sometimes is very effective. Care must be taken when covering the outside of the egg so that no creases or folds are visible.

It is possible to buy plastic shells in a limited variety of cuts and these could be quite useful to practise and experiment on if you can't get goose eggs. However, no self-respecting experienced egg crafter would dream of using one!

I make these little flower baskets as Easter gifts. The two side panels are cut away from a goose egg, leaving a basket shape with a handle. The handle is fragile and has to be treated with care.

The whole basket is covered with gold mesh stretched around the handle and glued underneath. The mesh is also stretched over the basket and glued into the bottom of the shell.

A little plaster of Paris adds weight inside the shell and this is covered with a piece of paper doyley. The flowers and butterfly are then arranged and glued into place. A white plastic curtain ring glued to the bottom of the shell stops the basket tipping over.

If you are adding a hinge, it has to be applied at this stage. It can either be covered with the fabric, or the trimming. If this does not appeal to you, you can disguise it with a small metal filigree or flat jewel. Apply with glue in the usual way, but make sure you do not glue up the hinge post, or the egg will not open and close!

Cut a square of material, enough to cover the section of shell you are covering. Cover the shell with a thin layer of white craft glue. Place the centre of the fabric squarely on top of the shell and stretch the material down over the curves, evenly spacing

any gathers or folds. The idea is to achieve a beautifully smooth finish. When the glue is dry, trim off the material to the edge of the shell, then cover any folds with braid or lace.

Unless cut or fabric edges are absolutely perfect these always have to be neatened and covered with braid, lace or cord. Nothing looks worse than an edging that doesn't quite meet, or overlaps thus giving a bulky appearance, so make sure your measurements are exact, or cut off the edging when it is fixed round the shell. This is particularly important when tackling larger eggs.

White craft glue is ideal for attaching edgings. Unless you have a syringe to apply the glue, use a cocktail stick and spread a thin line of adhesive, a section at a time, at the very edge of the shell, or where the braid or cord is to be applied. When it is tacky, attach the edging. If you are making a simple jewel box, start at the hinge on one side and work round to the other side of the hinge. Repeat on the other half shell. If you are making a more complicated design, or attaching fine cord round filigreed cuts, start at the back of the egg and work round carefully until you meet the cord again at the back, matching curves. Always start and end the braid where the join will be least visible, and in most cases this will be the hinge area. The two ends should butt together so that the join is virtually invisible.

An easy and effective way of decorating simple blown and painted Christmas or Easter eggs is to add a contrasting ribbon around the shell. Or decorate them with strips of velvet or lace.

When making up your own designs, try alternating rows of tiny pearls and cord, or experiment with rows of different sizes and styles of braids to give a pleasing effect. Always 'try' things on the shell before gluing them on. What seems like a good idea in theory doesn't always look so good in reality!

Decoupage

Decoupage entails the cutting out of various pictures, or parts of pictures, which are assembled on wood rather like a collage. These are then 'sunk' by means of many coats of varnish, sanding down between each layer. Boxes and small tables are decorated in this way. Decoupage is extremely popular and can be applied to this craft in the same way.

Choose a picture that you like from a greetings card, magazine or even wrapping paper. The thinner the paper the better. Cut out the image you have chosen and glue it to your prepared egg with craft glue. Wipe away any excess glue and when the paper is dry apply several coats of varnish, sanding between each layer. Apply the layers of varnish over the shell and the cut out print until the picture 'sinks' into the shell and no edge can be felt.

Transfers

There are many pretty transfers to be found and if you want your work to be individual you can even make your own. Shells can be covered quickly and easily and this is an ideal method of decoration if your painting skills are non-existent!

Prepare and paint the shell with enamels, (see page 34). A transfer is semi-transparent, so any base colour, other than white, will affect the tone of the transfer. Have a bowl of water, a soft cloth and a cotton wool bud ready. Lay the transfer, picture uppermost, on to the surface of the water. The water will soak through the paper backing and release the transfer; this should take approximately thirty seconds. Do not allow the transfer to separate completely and float away. As soon as it is loose, lift it, on its paper backing, out of the water. Holding the transfer close to the shell, slide just a little on to the exact area you have decided upon. Gripping the egg firmly, hold down this part of the transfer with your thumb and gently slide the paper backing down and away, keeping the transfer flat to the shell. Mop up any surplus water with absorbent paper. Now, with your cotton wool bud, work with a small circular motion from the centre outwards, pressing any air bubbles or creases to the outer edges. If a bad crease has developed, it is possible to lift that part of the transfer, providing it is still wet enough; re-position it, smoothing out as before with the cotton wool bud or your finger.

The transfer now has to be fixed on to the shell. This can be done by applying varnish, but do not apply the varnish directly on to the transfer, since in most cases it will crack. First, paint over the transfer with white glue thinned with a little water if necessary, so that it goes on smoothly. This will act as a barrier. Apply two coats to be on the safe side and allow to dry. Using a compatible varnish to your base paint (a clear enamel varnish if enamels have been used), apply two or three coats to the transfer and the shell, allowing each coat to dry well between applications. In this way the transfer becomes part of the shell; the edges of the transfer can neither be seen nor felt.

You can, of course, make your own transfers, from wrapping paper with pretty repeat designs, and greetings cards. Magazine prints are all right, providing the paper is not glossy. Choose small pictures to complement the size of your shell. There is a solution specially made for lifting prints, but I find acrylic medium, available from art shops, does the job equally well.

Cut out your chosen print, leaving a reasonable border all round, and tape it face up to a work board, or a piece of brown paper. This is just to keep it steady whilst working. Taking a large soft brush, dip it into the acrylic medium and paint strokes over the print in one direction only i.e. top to bottom or side to side, until it is coated with a thin film. Leave it to dry for at least fifteen minutes, or until it looks clear. Apply a second coat, but this time

This little quail egg requires very careful treatment as the shell is so thin.

I start by gluing a small flower and leaf print on to the shell and applying two coats of varnish; this gives strength to the fragile shell. Using a power tool and the smallest disc and a diamond flame drill, parts of the shell are then cut away around the print.

Using a space in the design, where there is a large enough gap to insert a brush, the interior is coated with glue and strengthened with ballentine. Parts of the design and all cut edges are picked out with the finest of old-gold metallic cord, before gluing tiny jewels to the flower centres. The egg is supported on a small gold stand.

in the opposite direction from the first application. Repeat this procedure, in alternate directions, for six coats. Leave to dry thoroughly, either all day or overnight.

The next stage requires great care, or the transfer will be torn. To soften the paper backing beneath the image, remove the print from the working surface and soak it for approximately fifteen minutes in a bowl of warm water. Remove the print from the water and using your fingers gently scratch, or rub away the paper backing. Re-soak it if it doesn't come away under gentle rubbing. A thick paper will require more soaking and will come off in layers before the acrylic film is reached. When most of the paper has been rubbed away, hold the remaining image (transfer) under a gently running tap, and very carefully slough off any remaining particles of paper. Take care not to stretch or tear the delicate film you now have in your hands. Cut away any parts of the transfer not required, making a neat edge round the image. It should be applied to the shell whilst still damp.

The home-made transfer looks cloudy when damp and it is not always easy to tell the right from wrong side. Be sure you place it right side up on the shell. If you do find it is reversed, it can be soaked off and re-applied correctly.

Apply a thin layer of white glue (diluted if necessary) to the area of shell where the print is to be placed. Lay the transfer on the shell and when it is positioned correctly smooth out any creases or air bubbles, working from the centre with your fingers and a soft cloth. The transfer can be stretched a little to fit the shell contour, but be careful not to tear it. When it is dry fix the transfer to the shell, using the method already described.

Raised paper flowers over a transfer

This technique gives a lovely three dimensional effect and enhances the beauty of a flat flower image. It is simple and extremely effective.

Choose three identical small flower prints; the repeat design on gift wrapping is ideal. Make a transfer as already described and apply it to the shell. Do not fix this base print with varnish at this stage.

Coat the second and third prints with four coats of acrylic medium and leave them to dry well. From these you will be building up the flower, cutting individual flowers, petals and leaves.

Start by layering up the largest flower, which is usually in the centre of the design. Using the second print that has been thickened with acrylic and very small, pointed scissors, cut from it individual flowers or petals.

Let us assume you have roses and daisies in the design. Daisies should be cut as a whole flower, separating the petals but leaving them attached to the centre. Place the cut-out flower face down

*A simple tilted horizontal cut
enables this duck egg to be set
almost upright on its stand.*

   *The egg shell is hinged at the top
so that the front lifts up. It is
decorated with a rose transfer with
an identical rose raised over it. The
cut edges are trimmed with a
simple looped braid.*

   *The red jewels were part of a
necklace, which I dismantled and
glued to the shell with strong fast-
drying adhesive.*

in the palm of your hand and with a small ball modelling tool, or
similar implement, press along each petal so they curve upwards
at their outer edges. When right way up the petals will curve
away from you at their outer edges. With a touch of glue, attach
the cut-out daisy centre on to the corresponding daisy you have
transferred on to the egg shell.

   Roses are built up by cutting out and layering individual petals.
First cut out the entire flowerhead from the print and make a
transfer for the shell. Then cut the individual petals, starting with
the longer outer ones and working in. Shape each petal with the
modelling tool as described and, with just a little glue on the edge
nearest the centre, fix to the corresponding part of the base

Two sheets of identical Christmas wrapping paper and cake decorations are used in the goose egg design shown on these two pages.

A large door is cut into each side of the shell. Attach the hinges to both doors; make two transfers from your chosen prints and apply to the shell doors. Raise flowers and leaves by cutting identical images from the second print and placing them over the base transfer. The robin's body is raised by cutting it out from the second print and padding it slightly with malleable plastic adhesive before gluing it to the base print.

A snow scene is painted inside the shell with watercolours. The outside is given four coats of high gloss hard-setting varnish. The red and white model church has been repainted and both the fir trees and the church have been sprinkled with diamond dust flakes.

The inside rims of the doors are edged with white velvet cord and the outside edged with gold. A gold tassle pull is sited exactly opposite each hinge on both sides. The design is complemented by a pretty gold stand.

flower. Roses have so many petals it may be necessary to use two prints, since in cutting one petal it is inevitable that you will take in part of another. Build up from the outside to the centre. Small flowers and leaves are cut out whole, shaped and added where required in the arrangement. Hold up the shell and look at it from all angles. If you can see the white backing paper anywhere it means the petal is too high. Gently flatten down the petal or give it more curve on the outer edge. The flowers will need hardening with several coats of varnish. Use a fine brush and thoroughly coat each petal and bloom, allowing each coat to dry well between applications.

Jewellery

All sorts of beads and pieces of jewellery can be used to adorn your egg. Egg craft suppliers stock a wide variety of beautiful accessories, but it is also worthwhile looking through your jewel box, or asking friends if they have any unwanted items. I have spent many happy hours browsing round junk shops and jumble sales, seeking just the right piece to complete a special design.

Small brooches make lovely finials; chains and pretty drop earrings can be transformed into door pulls or handles; rows of pearls can be used to frame a picture. If there is no blow hole in the bottom of the shell, and if it suits the style you have created,

The cut for this lovely silver jewel box created from a goose egg, is described on page 25. A gunmetal grey, 1960s' earring is used effectively to complete the design. It is glued to the top of the egg with strong, fast-drying adhesive.

Blown quail eggs form the basis of five of the pendants shown opposite.

From left to right, the first shell is left in its natural state. It is given several coats of varnish for strength. After sanding down the last coat of varnish, white clear-drying craft glue is applied and the shell is covered completely with ballentine. A coat of varnish is then applied, a bell cap is fixed to the top and a jump ring is used to join the neck chain to the bell. It is finished with a gold tassle drop.

The second egg is a Fabergé design. The entire egg is covered with modelling material into which markings are impressed, before baking it in the oven. Blue acrylic paint is used before varnishing and rhinestones and gold cord are added as a finishing touch.

The top egg is completely covered with pearls and rhinestones. These are attached to the blown shell with strong, fast-drying glue. The egg is dipped several times into heavy clear varnish and allowed to dry between coats. This is continued until the jewels 'sink' into the varnish and the outside is smooth.

The fourth pendant is simple, but elegant. Several coats of emerald green paint are applied to the shell to achieve a deep, even colour. The entire egg is covered with ballentine and then varnished. Bell caps are fixed top and bottom before attaching the tassle and neck chain.

The last quail egg is covered entirely with a tiny flower print. If the paper is thin enough you don't need to make a transfer. Tiny flowers on a second print are then cut out and raised slightly and glued over the base print. Several coats of varnish are needed to strengthen and harden the design; a tassle and neck chain are then added.

The flat pendant frame in the centre contains a painted piece of goose shell. Using the frame as a template, draw the shape on to a piece of shell. Sand around the edges until it fits perfectly into the frame. I have painted a miniature of primroses in watercolours but you could use a transfer of tiny flowers or a scene. A delicate braid hides the join between frame and shell. The back of the shell piece is filled with plaster of Paris and covered with thin velvet.

leave the shell plain. But, if there is a hole cover it with a sequin, or do something more exciting. When creating Christmas tree eggs, (see page 73), thread various beads, crystals or pearls on to a long pin, ending with a gold or silver bead cap and glue them over the hole.

Remember, always 'try' things on the shell before gluing them on. Once you have decided on your design, apply the stones and beads to your egg with craft glue, wiping away any excess, then leave to dry.

Lettering

As my calligraphy is not up to standard, I always use the transfer variety of lettering on my designs, when adding dates, initials or well-known phrases and sayings. This type of lettering is available from most art shops.

Paint the egg in the usual way and before varnishing apply the lettering to the shell, rubbing over each letter carefully with a pencil. When you have finished, seal the lettering by applying a coat of thinned down clear glue. When this is dry, the varnish can be applied to the whole egg.

I have used another method on the following page, which is just as effective. The whole oval showing the butterfly, flower and

55

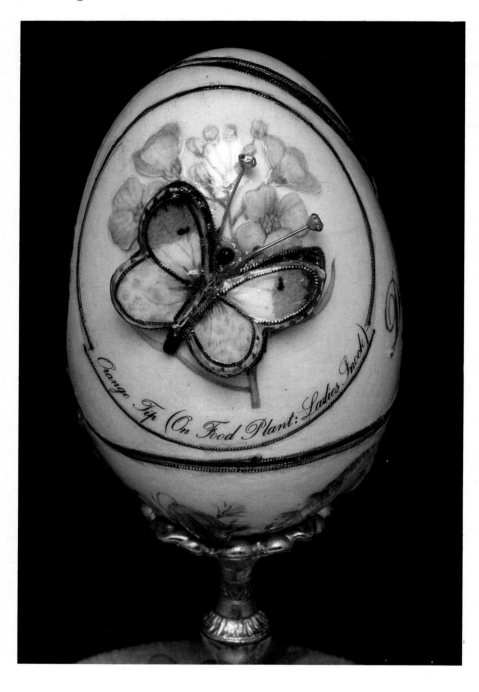

This beautiful butterfly music box was made for my parents' fiftieth wedding anniversary.

The goose egg shell is left in its natural state and not painted. Two panels are cut into the shell and hinged before the egg is decorated.

Motifs are taken from three identical sheets of gift wrap paper; this design shows lettering below a pretty pattern. Two transfers are made of the design, one for the front and one for the back. They are applied to each of the two large cut panels. Other flower transfers are applied to the base shell. The flowers, leaves and butterflies are raised using identical prints.

The wings on the butterfly illustrated here actually move. If you want to create a 'working' butterfly a special hinge is used with a long post that extends beyond the sides of the hinge.

After the transfer has been applied to the shell, cut a slot along the body of the butterfly through the shell just the length of the hinge. Using strong fast-drying adhesive glue the hinge on to the wings on both sides, making sure the hinge post is set into the pre-cut slot and that no glue seeps anywhere near the hinge post.

When the glue is set, carefully cut out the shell around the butterfly transfer with a craft drill; hopefully the hinge will work freely and hold the wings up. Cut out a matching butterfly and cover the cut-out butterfly, thus hiding the hinge. Apply four coats of varnish to the cut-out butterfly.

The area beneath the cut-out butterfly and the egg interior is lined with gold mesh. Once the varnish has dried on the butterfly, glue it back on to the shell with a touch of adhesive at the tips of the elongated hinge post.

The music box, with a platform key, is set into a velvet covered sweet jar lid. The egg stand is glued to this platform key. The egg turns round as the music plays.

lettering at the front of the egg, was 'lifted' from a quality gift wrap using the transfer method described on page 49. As the background to the print was white, this blended well with the rest of the design and colour, once the egg was painted and varnished. The '50' shown on the side of the egg was applied using the transfer method.

Pens and inks can be used, but this is rather specialised and I find beautiful results can be achieved using the above two methods.

The two doors in this goose egg fold down flat to reveal hikers who have just stumbled upon a crystal cave. Miniature railway models, trees and ground cover were invaluable in creating this design.

Everything fixed in the two doors has to be strategically placed so that items don't collide when the doors are closed up! The centre of the egg contains plaster rocks and a waterfall. The waterfall is made of tissue paper dipped into clear glue and fixed in folds from top to bottom of one side of the cave. Once set, several more layers of glue are spread down the tissue so that it drips into a pond at the base. The delicate strands suspended from the roof are tiny grasses dipped into ballentine.

The closed egg is decorated with pressed flowers on a blue-green enamelled shell and is set on a wooden base.

This egg was a competition prize-winner.

Models and miniatures

Beautiful scenes can be created inside an egg simply using a little imagination, some paints, and a few models and miniatures. The egg shown on the opposite page opens up to reveal two young ramblers walking through a shady grotto. The dried miniature flowers and grasses add depth and dimension to the scene.

Models can be bought, or you can make your own if you have a particular idea in mind. Use the bread dough recipe on page 61, or there are a variety of modelling compounds that are suitable. Air drying clay can be bought in most craft shops and painted with acrylics or poster paint when dry; or I use a modelling compound which is hardened in the oven. This comes in a variety of colours and pack sizes and is also found in most craft shops. The different coloured packs can be used according to your colour scheme, or the models can be made in white and then painted in the usual way. Follow the baking instructions on the packet, but since the models are so tiny, be careful not to burn them!

Dried grasses and miniature flowers can be bought from most florists and they add colour and realism to any scene. Choose colours to complement your design and make sure they are in scale.

I design my scene first and then paint my backdrop on the inside of the shell. I always work from the back to the front, gluing each piece into position with touches of white craft glue. Don't be afraid to experiment. Anything goes, as long as it is not too large or heavy!

A little duck floats serenely on a mirror pond surrounded by miniature flowers and grasses. The country scene is painted on to the goose egg interior with acrylics and the pond is supported by plaster of Paris, which also adds weight to the egg.

A similar cut is used here as is used on the goose girl egg shown on page 35. Measure and mark the shell very carefully before starting any cutting. A goose egg forms the base of this design.

The top of the egg is covered with gold mesh and a bell cap with a jump ring is glued solidly to the top. The openings are completely covered with heavy metallic braid and edged with a much finer braid on either side.

There is a thin layer of plaster of Paris in the base of the shell. The egg is filled with an arrangement of bread dough daffodils.

Finally, a gold tassle is glued to the base of the egg, and the whole thing is suspended from a hanging stand.

Bread dough flowers

Beautiful bread dough flowers can be made cheaply and simply, and they look very effective both on the outsides and insides of eggs. A posy of tiny blossoms set inside a shell with a flower theme can be a delight and I find roses and daisies are particularly appealing.

Icing cakes and decorating eggs may seem to be totally unconnected, but this is a prime example of how another art form can be adapted and used in your work. Having decorated cakes for many years, I stumbled across a recipe for modelling icing containing gelatine, which enabled me to make very thin petals for roses and other flowers. Thinking that what worked with icing sugar might work equally as well with bread dough, I experimented and found the added gelatine did in fact enable me to make beautifully delicate flowers. There are many moulds and flower cutters used with modelling icing that can also be used to great effect with bread dough. However, if you want your work to be individual you can make your own. I find this gives more personal satisfaction anyway. The recipe I use is shown below, followed by details of how to make a rose. Experiment and use this method to create other flowers.

RECIPE

6 slices of bread from a medium-sliced loaf, with crusts cut off. It needs to be on the stale side, so if you have just bought it, leave the slices out in the air for an hour or two.
3 tablespoons white craft glue
1 tablespoon white acrylic paint
1 teaspoon gelatine
1 teaspoon glycerine
2/3 drops lemon juice

Break the bread into small pieces in a bowl, or give it a quick spin in a good liquidiser. I know some who make up the entire dough in a liquidiser, but it does make an awful mess. I wonder if the cleaning up afterwards makes it worthwhile! I have always made mine by hand, in a glass or plastic container.

Dissolve the gelatine according to the packet instructions. Combine all the ingredients and mix with a spoon. When the mixture starts coming together, leaving the sides of the bowl comparatively clean, take it out and continue kneading it in your hands. Do put the bowl and spoon in to soak as soon as you have finished or the glue and acrylic will set hard. Keep working the dough until it is no longer sticky and has become smooth and pliable. It is now ready for use and must be stored in an airtight plastic bag or it will dry out. Kept in the fridge it will remain usable for several weeks.

ROSE

Only remove from the bag as much dough as you require and keep the rest well sealed. Think miniature! Aim at delicate porcelain-like flower heads. If the first ones turn out too large but look good, instead of reserving them for egg designs, make an arrangement in a pretty little pot with some dried foliage and they will still be admired.

Gather together some hand lotion or talcum powder to stop

your hands getting sticky, cocktail sticks and white glue. If you want stems you will need flower wires and green florists' tape. If flower heads only are going to be arranged on the shell, they can be dried on cocktail sticks and then removed. Use a pot filled with clay to support the flowers while they are drying.

Take a ball of dough the size of a small pea. Press it out between finger and thumb, so it is no bigger than 0.5 cm (¼in) in diameter. Make three of these. Lay them on the work surface slightly overlapping each other with the merest touch of glue to hold them.

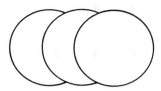

overlap bread dough petals

Starting at one end, roll them up like a swiss roll to form a bud. If you are adding a stem, wrap the flower wire in green tape, then dip the end into some craft glue and push a little way into the base of the bud; pinch the dough at the base to grip the stem. If no stem is required, just push the bud on to the cocktail stick. Use the clay as a support and leave in a warm place to dry. This could take six to eight hours, so make several buds at the same time.

form a bud and attach stem

Make three or four more petals in the same manner, thinning out the top edge with finger and thumb just a little. Attach each one slightly overlapping, with a little glue, to the base of the bud. Ensure that each row of petals is on and not below the bud, or it will take on a conical appearance. Allow to dry.

Once more add three or four more petals to the outside. These should be pressed into a more oval shape and just a little longer than the original petals. The ultimate aim is to make the flowers look as life-like as possible and photographs, or studies of the real thing, are invaluable. Shape the petals before they dry by curving them under or over in a realistic way.

right way of attaching petals

To make the leaves, take another large pea-sized piece of dough and press out to an approximate leaf shape. Using a real or plastic leaf, press it into the dough to create the veins. Cut the leaf to size, shape and glue it to a wire and let it dry.

Bread dough takes several days to dry. Place your models in the airing cupboard to quicken the drying process, before painting.

wrong way of attaching petals

When it comes to colouring the flowers there are two methods you can use. If you wish, you can add watercolour or tempera to the dough, working and kneading it in. This gives a uniform colour throughout. Alternatively, paint the flowers after they are dry, using watercolours or acrylic paints. This is the method I prefer and with a photograph before me, I use colours as near as possible to the real flower. I use a very fine paintbrush to get in between the petals and start with pale washes building up the colours. When the dry flower is painted it will absorb moisture which must be allowed to dry out. So, leave the painted flowers in a dust-free environment to dry out thoroughly, before finishing by coating with a clear nail varnish. Store in tissue paper in a box

press the dough into a leaf

Many different flowers can be made out of bread dough. The picture here shows an enchanting bouquet of modelled flowers.

The flowers can be coloured before modelling by adding small amounts of paint to the dough; detail can be added later. Or the flowers can be painted after they dry using either watercolours or acrylics. Use photographs of real flowers to match colours and details. A glaze is added to give a porcelain-like finish.

until you use them. Examples of bread dough flowers can be seen above and on page 60. They can be applied to the shell with ordinary craft glue.

You can do almost anything in bread dough that can be done with commercial modelling materials as long as the model is not too large. Try your hand at simple animals, rabbits, hedgehogs and so on. The dough model must be absolutely dry throughout before it is varnished and thereby sealed. If it isn't it will eventually rot and crumble to pieces.

Weighting the egg

I usually complete all exterior decorations, apart from the finial and the stand, before going on to the next stage, which is to weight the egg. Obviously not all eggs can be weighted, only those that have been cut to expose shell interiors. But where you can it is wise to carry out this stage. By making the egg a little heavier it will make it more stable, so that it will stand more chance of surviving accidental knocks or being blown over. I have known people place their gift eggs near an open window within the reach of billowing curtains and good-bye egg!

To weight down the shell I use plaster, but clay, or even lead fishing weights mixed with epoxy, will do. Sit the egg upright in an egg box, or other suitable container, to keep it steady. If you are using clay, take a walnut-sized piece and shape it to the contours of the bottom of the egg, flattening the top. Glue it into the egg with adhesive. If using lead weights, mix with glue and leave them to set in the bottom of the egg.

If using plaster of Paris, put a heaped tablespoon in a plastic pot and, stirring all the time, add cold water to make a creamy consistency. Have the egg ready, well supported in a box, and immediately pour in the plaster. Don't use too much as it generates a certain amount of heat and can crack the shell; about 2 cm (¾in) in an average goose egg is about right. Leave the egg open and set aside to dry out overnight. Plaster firms up almost immediately, so do have everything ready and be prepared to work quickly and cleanly.

Lining the egg

There are many ways of completing the inside of the egg. Materials such as satin, silk and velvet give a luxurious look. For those handy with a needle the linings could offer an interesting challenge, such as pleats or tiny cushions. The following method is simple yet effective and is the method employed for a basic jewel box.

The material needs to be fine and soft so that it will naturally fall into attractive folds. Never forget that you are working with a fragile egg shell. If you are lining a jewel box, fold the two halves as far back as the hinge will allow and at no time put undue pressure on the hinge. If you have arrived at this stage without disaster, be encouraged by knowing that the more you put on or in the egg, the more the shell gradually increases in strength.

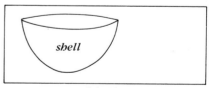

fabric cut on the cross

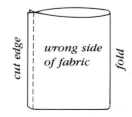

Cut an oblong piece of material on the cross. It should be equal in depth to the section of the shell you are lining and as wide as the shell rim circumference plus 1 cm (½in). With the 'right' side on the inside, fold the material in half and sew the side edges together to form a tube. Turn the material back to the right side.

I love penguins and this bought model of a little penguin and her egg is quite delightful.

A simple vertically cut goose egg is hinged and then watercolours are used to paint penguins sitting on ice floes around the shell. Plaster of Paris is built up in layers in the base of the shell and painted; this serves the dual purpose of adding weight and providing a snowy base for the model. Plaster is also poured over a piece of granite stone for the egg to stand on.

Diamond dust and ballentine are applied here and there to provide a touch of sparkle to the snowy scene. Fix the egg to the base with a fair amount of strong fast-setting glue.

Place a line of white glue around the inside rim of the shell. The glue should not be too thick, but it can be spread approximately 0.5 cm (¼in) down into the shell all around. Now you have to attach 0.5 cm (¼in) of one end of the tube to the top inside of the shell. The tube is more controllable if the material is pulled over the middle three fingers of the right hand if right-handed, left hand if left-handed. Wait until the glue is tacky. The seam of the material should be in line with the hinge, or opposite at the front, where it will be less obvious. Spread the fingers so that the material is taut and, lowering the tips of the fingers supporting the bottom edge of material into the egg, manoeuvre the tube to touch the glue here and there. When it is in place, run your finger around the rim, fixing *all* the material to the shell. Distribute any folds evenly round the rim as it is glued in place.

Working through the tube of material, drop some white glue into the bottom of the shell, spreading it around a little. Fold and gather in the top raw edges of the material pushing in the corners of the tube to give a more rounded appearance. Either glue, or lightly stitch together. As soon as this is done, push the material down into the egg. Using a cocktail stick, move the folds around until the lining looks attractive. Press here and there, enabling the glue to hold the lining in place. The material should be pushed far enough down the shell so that none of it stands above the rim, thus impeding the full closure of the jewel box, or whichever design you are lining. If necessary repeat the whole procedure on the other half of the egg. Neaten off the edges with a row of narrow braid around the top inside edge of the shell.

Fitting a trace chain

A trace chain must be fitted if the hinge is slack, to stop the lid of an egg falling right back when opened, so over-balancing the egg. If the hinge stays put wherever it is and the decorations are not too heavy, this may not always be necessary.

Using silver or gold fine chain to suit the design, cut off a suitable length. Be on the generous side. If it is too short the lid will not stay open. The exact measurement will vary from egg to egg, but a rough guide would be to open the shell as wide as shown in the illustration opposite and measure the distance at its longest, i.e. the front of the shell. Although the trace chain will not be fixed at the front, this measurement will allow for the extra length required for gluing. If in doubt always cut longer, especially for the first attempt. The chain will be sited approximately halfway between centre front and the side. If it is too near the front it will become an unwanted focal point; if it is too near the side it will fall to the outside of the egg every time the shell

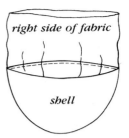

right side of fabric

shell

glue the fabric to the inside shell edge

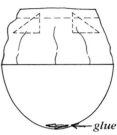

glue

gather and stitch the fabric

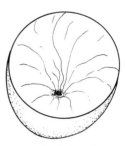

push the fabric into the egg

A quail egg is cut in half to make this tiny jewel box which is enlarged in this photograph. Cut carefully as these eggs are so fragile.

Four coats of emerald green enamel are applied to the exterior and interior and the two halves are then lined with gold mesh material before hinging together with a tiny but firm hinge. Gold cord and braid are fixed round the rims covering the hinge. The egg is glued to a bright gold petal stand.

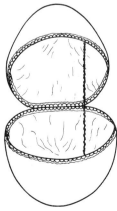

correct position for a trace chain

is closed. Situated halfway between, it should drop freely inside when the jewel box is shut.

You will need epoxy rapid glue, the inevitable cocktail stick, plus a bowl of water and a towel ready for a quick clean up should your fingers get sticky whilst working.

Glue the trace chain to the lid first. Gently ease the cocktail stick down between the lining and the shell, at the point where the chain is to be glued in. The shell membrane will probably come away with the material, but that doesn't matter. What you are doing is making a little pocket in which the chain will be fixed. Mix up a small amount of epoxy, and again using the cocktail stick, drop a little inside the pocket. Feed in about

67

0.5 cm (¼in) of chain, using the stick to keep the pocket open. Press the lining back into place to secure the chain. Hold it there for a minute or two. Hopefully no glue has oozed out over the edge of the shell, but if it has remove with a wet craft knife after the chain is sufficiently well fixed, (approximately five minutes), so as not to dislodge it. Lay the egg down while the glue is setting.

Once the chain is quite secure, make a pocket as before in the lower half of the shell, opposite the one above. Ensure that the chain is straight down from top to bottom and free from twists and kinks. Mix up some more epoxy and glue the chain into the opening as before, bearing in mind the length of chain needed to allow the lid to remain wide open. Always check that the egg will close properly after each of these procedures. If the chain seems to impede closure, ease it away from the shell a little. Keep checking to make sure the egg will close and make any final adjustments before the glue dries too hard.

Stands

When choosing a stand, not only should it be the right colour, but also the style and height to complement the egg. Although there are always exceptions to every rule, a horizontal-cut shell would not look at home on a tall thin stand. Similarly, a large upright jewel box egg would, in most cases, look unhappy on a small squat stand; rather a tall stand would add elegance and style. A silver trimmed shell would not look right on a gold stand, whereas an egg that was decorated with a mixture of silver and gold would probably look alright. The type of stand that has a shallow cup for the egg to sit in is the easiest from the gluing point of view. Other kinds are variations on the three-legged theme which means that the fixing has to be very precise.

Most of my nature theme eggs I place on pieces of bark, or other natural material. What goes on, in and under the egg, must all be pleasing to the eye. If you want your work to be unique, it is worthwhile looking around junk shops and jumble sales for interesting pieces of jewellery, materials and unusual objects that can be converted into stands.

Always use epoxy rapid glue for fixing the egg to the stand. The last thing you want, after all your efforts, is to have the egg and stand part company, just as you are proudly showing off your accomplishments to friends and family.

To take a 'cup' stand as an example, spread a layer of epoxy round the inside and, viewing at eye level, place the egg as straight and upright as possible into the cup. If you are attaching a three-legged stand, place one leg at the centre back of the egg. You will then have two legs towards the front. If on the other hand the stand is a three-legged reversible one, great care must

At the time that I made this egg I had never seen anything similar, so it was all very much trial and error. All I knew was that I wanted an egg to open up into a flower. I decided on an Art Nouveau style magnolia blossom, and from my collection of shells chose the largest, longest goose egg I could find plus one of a similar shape, but smaller, to fit inside.

Each shell is cut into three petals, leaving a section of shell to form the base. They are then hinged back together to form the flower.

The inner egg is painted with acrylics and the petals coated inside and out with ballentine. The inside is part-filled with plaster and covered with dark green velvet on which sits a frosted glass bird.

The outer shell is covered in gesso, including the hinges, which gives texture and interest to the exterior when the egg is fully closed. The shell is then painted with acrylics and varnished.

The outside petal interiors are lined with dark green soft taffeta. The inner shell has to be lifted high enough to allow the petals to open up between the outside shell petals. To do this I put gradual layers of plaster into the base of the outer shell until the correct height is achieved. The inner egg is then glued into position.

The completed flower is glued firmly to a tall elegant stand which in turn is attached to a velvet covered wooden plinth.

Many beautiful and varied designs can be carried out with just one basic cut. Here the vertical jewel box idea is converted into a pot pourri container using a goose egg.

The flower design is painted straight on to the shell which is then varnished. The interior is not lined; if the membrane inside is intact and clean you need only varnish; if not then apply two or three coats of enamel paint. Drill a few holes in the lid to allow the scent of the dried petals to escape and then hinge the two shell halves together. Place a layer of plaster of Paris in the base of the shell and paint over it.

The egg is latched so that the pot pourri can't tip out even when the egg is picked up. The latch is glued on with strong fast-drying adhesive, exactly opposite the hinge at the back. Bend the ends of the latch to match the curve of the shell. Glue the top part into place near the rim, and when set, mark where the lower half is to be glued so that it will latch down properly.

The egg is trimmed with Russian braid and is set on a pretty gold stand.

be taken in applying the glue as there will be only three small touch points.

Place a small amount of glue on the stand, only where it will touch the shell. When the egg is on the stand there will be a few minutes for adjustment during the drying process. Again, viewing at eye level, turn the stand with the egg in place and assure yourself that it is straight from all angles. Make any minor adjustments before the epoxy sets hard.

If the stand is a piece of bark or rock, centre the egg and keep it as upright as you can. Cork bark is available from florists, but it is cheaper to find your own. Wash the bark thoroughly, then when dry preserve it by painting on several coats of wood glue.

Hanging eggs can look particularly effective, (see page 15), and they do not need to be weighted. The stands usually end in a hook, through which a loop can be fed. You will need a large up-eye threaded through with a jump ring, (available from most jewellery accessory suppliers). Glue the up-eye to the top of the egg with epoxy rapid. Wait until it is dry and set hard, then attach the egg to the stand.

Finishing touch

Finials can be bought or they can be invented from bits and bobs of jewellery. They are the final touch on the top of a jewelled or upright egg. If you feel your design would be enhanced by a crowning jewel, or beautiful ornate finial, glue it into position with strong fast-drying glue.

Projects

I have now covered all the techniques needed to make simple and more complicated designs. The projects in this section range from simple blown egg ideas for Christmas, to a more complicated picture egg which is one of my favourites—Sleeping Beauty. Whatever the size or design, I get the same amount of pleasure out of this craft. I hope you do too. Try the simple projects at the beginning of this section before creating your own masterpiece!

Christmas tree decorations

Many attractive eggs can be made from simple blown hen or duck shells. Christmas tree baubles make lovely gifts and they are easy enough to make for bazaars or sales. They can be as simple or as intricate as you wish.

In the case of Christmas tree eggs, shells can be mass-produced by spraying all the shells the same colour before adding similar ornamentation to each. Buy lots of glitter and sparkle. You can go a bit over the top with bright festive decorations and they will be beautifully displayed against the Christmas tree lights.

Materials

Lengths of ribbon, cord and beading will vary, according to the size of the eggs, so no exact measurements are given. Measure the circumference of the eggs to work out approximate lengths required.

Blown hen, bantam or small duck eggs; gold, silver, red, green or other suitable colour aerosol spray paints, or enamels; craft glue; glitter; sequins; narrow velvet ribbon; various lengths of contrasting ribbon; gold and silver cord; beads, crystals and strings of small pearls; bottle tops; Christmas transfers or prints; up-eyes (these are available from most jewellery accessory suppliers and are used on hanging eggs); varnish; knitting needle or thin stick; drying rack, (see page 34); egg box.

72

Beautiful Christmas tree decorations can be created using simple blown hen and duck eggs. The shells can be painted and varnished, or covered with glitter and braid.

'Hot air balloons' are a firm favourite with children and little gold-covered presents can be hidden inside the baskets, ready for Christmas day.

A variety of simple cuts can be used to reveal festive interiors. The shells are cut, then coated in craft glue and sparkling glitter. Tiny angels and sprigs of holly peep out through braid-edged windows.

A seasonal transfer is used to decorate the uncut shell on the far right. After varnishing, gold braid, pearls and glitter are added with strong fast-drying glue.

Projects

Method

Either spray your eggs with paint, (see page 36), or use the enamel paints and the marbling technique, (see page 34).

Once your eggs are dry you can start adorning them with festive decorations. A simple and effective way of decorating tree eggs is to just add contrasting narrow velvet ribbon, or a wide ribbon, horizontally around the shell, with a flat bow and a long loop for hanging.

Transfers and small seasonal pictures add charm to a festive egg. For details of this technique see pages 49–54. Pictures can be framed with silver or gold braid. Sequins and tiny beads would add a lovely touch; these can be applied to the painted shell using touches of craft glue. Let your imagination run riot!

Small eggs can be completely covered in glitter, or freehand random designs can be drawn on to the shell with glue and glitter. Have a box handy to catch the surplus glitter. Hold the shell by passing a long thin stick, or knitting needle, through the blow hole, and squeeze thick white craft glue in random patterns over the painted surface of the shell. Sprinkle the glitter quite thickly over the glue and tap lightly to shake off the excess into the box. Allow to dry for several hours then shake off any loose glitter. The simple rack shown on page 34 is ideal for this drying process.

To complete the tops and bottoms of your eggs, you will need

A festive transfer trimmed with braid and a sprig of frosted holly decorate these hen eggs. Glitter and pearls are added to complete the designs.

Here is another way to complete a 'hot air balloon'. Red and gold enamel paints decorate the egg and the top of the shell is covered with ballentine. Thin gold braid frames the design and lengths of gold chain are used to represent the ropes. The basket is covered with beads and gold braid.

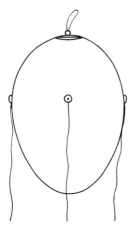

attach the four cords to the shell

something by which to hang them from the tree and something to cover the blow hole, if you have not already done so with ribbon or other decoration. If the hole is at the top, glue on an up-eye and thread some thin cord through it for hanging. Using an up-eye gives a professional look, but if you can't find any use the following method.

Cut a 13 cm (5in) to 15 cm (6in) length of fine cord and knot it into a loop. Glue the knot into the hole and when secure, cover with a sequin or other complementary jewel. A strong white craft glue is suitable for these eggs since the shells are lightweight, but do allow each stage to dry thoroughly.

If there is no hole in the bottom of the egg and you are pleased with it without any added decorations, just leave it plain. If there is a hole, cover it with a sequin or do something more exciting. Beads, crystals or pearls can be threaded on a long pin capped with a gold or silver bead and glued over the hole. Look through your jewellery box; you may find a piece of necklace or a pretty drop earring that will do beautifully.

'Hot air balloon' eggs are a favourite and are simple to make. If the basket contains a quality chocolate, or other small gift, the whole thing makes an original present from the tree to friends, especially the unexpected ones that arrive bearing small gifts at Christmas time! You will need a painted egg, strings of small pearls or other beads and gold or silver cord. For the basket I use small and large bottle tops from soft drink bottles. You will also need some braid or velvet ribbon wide enough to cover the bottle top.

Choose a fairly round hen or duck egg. Use egg boxes or egg cups to support your shells, either upright or on their sides, whilst parts are setting or drying. Whatever the shape of the egg keep the more pointed end facing downwards. Start by gluing your up-eye on to the top of your egg with craft glue. Thread the thin cord through the up-eye. This will provide you with a 'handle' to work with.

Cut four pieces of gold or silver cord, each approximately 10 cm (4in) long. These will form the 'ropes' from which the basket will hang. All measurements can only be approximate as they depend entirely on the size and shape of the egg. Now you have to glue on each length of cord to the sides of the egg, about two-thirds of the way up.

Take the first piece of cord and, using a touch of glue, attach it to the shell so that it hangs loose, except where it is actually glued to the egg. Do not be impatient. Let each part set before you go on to the next and lay the shell on its side or you will find the glue and the cords will slide down the shell and stick in all the wrong places. When dry, glue the next piece, exactly opposite the first length of cord, on the other side of the egg. Repeat this procedure with the other two pieces, so that all four lengths are equidistant around the shell. Glue suitable coloured sequins to cover the ends of the cords attached to the shell.

For the next stage you will need strings of pearls or beads, or soft cord that will drape nicely. Two or three loops can be hung around the shell. Starting at one sequin, lay the pearls or cord against the shell and measure them as you loop them, making a soft curve to the next sequin. When you are satisfied cut off, then measure three more lengths the same. Attach the first loop at each end with craft glue right up to each sequin. Repeat with the other three lengths. Either stop at this stage or add one or two more rows of pearls or cord, but make each set of loops deeper.

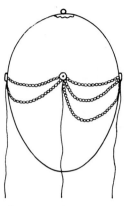

loop pearls around the shell

Now for the basket. Paint the bottle top with enamels, inside and out, to match the egg. When dry, spread a thin layer of glue inside and coat with glitter. Wait until it is dry and shake out the surplus.

Attaching the bottle top to the four cords is the most frustrating part since it must hang level. You cannot be sure of this until you hold the egg up; if you do this while the glue is too wet the bottle top will slide off! It needs to hang about 2.5 cm (1in) to 4 cm (1½in) below the egg.

Draw a line of glue down the outside of the bottle top and place it on your work table. Hold the egg above it and when the glue is tacky stick the first cord 'rope' to the 'basket', at a distance that looks right to you. If the cords are too long they can be cut off when all four have been fixed. Don't worry if the outside of the bottle top gets a bit messy since it will be covered with braid and rough areas won't show. When the first cord is secure, attach the next one on the opposite side.

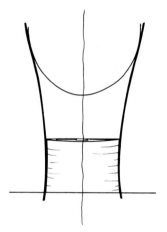

glue the cords to the bottle top

With the basket still resting on the table, hold the egg up so that both lengths of cord are taut; adjust while the glue is still tacky. When satisfied, lay the egg down beside the bottle top, being careful not to pull the cords; leave to set. Repeat with the two remaining cords. Hold your 'balloon' up before the glue is completely dry and make any minor adjustments by moving the last two cords slightly up or down.

Finally cover the 'basket' with velvet ribbon, or fancy braid. Nothing looks worse than ribbon or braid that does not quite meet or overlaps thus giving a bulky appearance, so measure your chosen material, making sure it meets edge to edge. If you are cutting braids that fray quickly, put a little glue on to the cutting line, allow to dry and when you cut you should have two clean crisp edges. Spread glue around the outside of the basket and stick on the braid or ribbon. Trim away any of the four cords that are hanging below the basket.

Your hot air balloon is now ready to hang on the Christmas tree. Don't forget to put a small gift in the basket! Children will love these novelty eggs and the hidden gift will bring great delight.

*Here, three elegantly simple eggs are cut as horizontal hinged jewel
boxes or Christmas gifts.*

*The design on the left is a goose egg. White/gold paint covers the shell
and gold metallic paint is used for the freehand design of stems and
leaves. Four coats of hard gloss varnish are used to give a perfect finish.
Gold pearls and braid decorate cut edges. This egg is a competition
prize-winner.*

*The goose egg on the right has a raised rose design drawn out with
gesso through a glue syringe. The entire shell is painted bright gold.
White/gold and platinum/gold paints accentuate parts of the flowers.
Gold braid is used to trim the edges.*

*The central duck egg has a slight variation on the straight horizontal
cut, in that it curves down both in the front and back of the design.
When half opened it resembles a seashell. Here only varnish is used to
enhance the shell and a simple gold pearl trim decorates the edges. The
interior is coated with pearl flakes to give strength and a simple
beauty.*

Bells

Many people collect handbells in brass, porcelain and glass, but few will have a bell made from an egg shell in their collection. Choose a large hen, duck, or preferably, goose egg. A torpedo shaped shell is best, so that the bell will be narrow at the handle and wide at the base. The cutting is simple but it must be exact or the bell will end up being lopsided.

Materials

As the shapes and sizes of eggs vary, it is impossible to give exact measurements or amounts of materials required.

Blown hen, duck or goose eggs; rubber band and pencil for marking the shell; hacksaw, or electric craft drill, mask and goggles for cutting the egg; sandpaper; enamel paints; cocktail stick; varnish; ballentine (optional); craft glue; rapid epoxy glue; 2 small bells (optional); 2 short lengths of fine, but sturdy, wire; 2 bell handles; transfer; bread dough flowers; string of gold beads; gold braid.

Method

Mark and cut your egg, using the straight cut technique described on page 23, drawing the pencil line around the fattest part of the shell. Then drill (or tap with a metal skewer) a hole in the top of the shell.

I always check that the bell is not lopsided after cutting the shell. The easiest way, I find, is to place the shell on a flat surface and look at it all around at eye-level. If it seems to be slightly up on one side use sandpaper to smooth away the cut edge of the shell until it is level with the flat surface.

Having cut the shell there are many decorative possibilities, (see pages 30 to 63). If you are painting your bell, prepare the shell by sanding down any rough areas (see page 33). If you are using a duck egg you may just want to apply a few coats of varnish to enhance the pretty colour of the shell.

The two bells illustrated opposite are simple, but effective. I start by deciding on my colours. I then wash and clean both shell interiors and I apply two coats of enamel paints to both shell interiors, to complement the exterior colours. You can apply ballentine if you have it, (see page 38), to add extra strength to the shells, or just apply a layer of varnish over the paint once it is dry.

Now I paint on my exterior colours. The bell on the right is painted with three coats of matt green enamel paint. Allow each coat to dry well in between applications. The finished surface should be smooth and perfect. The other bell is also enamelled, but here I used the marbling technique described on page 34, with white and pale green paints. Once the paints were dry I

These two goose egg bells would make an attractive and unusual gift for a friend or relative. The cutting is simple, but it has to be exact or the bell will not 'stand' properly.

White and pale green enamel paints are mixed to produce a marbled effect and painted on to the bell on the left. Once the paints are dry, a layer of ballentine is applied to create a pretty three dimensional effect. Bread dough flowers decorate the shell and gold braid trims the bottom edge. A tiny bell sits inside the shell, which is strengthened with ballentine, and a brass handle completes the design.

Three coats of matt green enamel paint cover the bell on the right. A Christmas transfer adds a festive feel; this is applied once the final coat of paint is quite dry, then the shell is covered with two coats of varnish. Gold beads and braid border the lower edge; a small bell sits inside the shell, which is strengthened with ballentine, and an elaborate brass handle completes the design.

twist the doubled up wire threaded through the bell loop

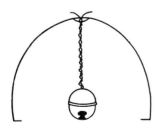

thread the wire through the hole in the top of the shell

applied a layer of ballentine. This gives a lustrous three dimensional effect which is very pretty.

The next stage is optional. You will need a small bell to make your large painted bell ring, but you don't have to put it in if you don't wish to. Most good pet shops will stock these little ringing bells. You will also need a length of fine, but sturdy, wire on which to suspend the little bell.

The bells need to hang about 1 cm (½in) above the rim of the shell. Take a piece of wire twice the length of the shell, thread it through the little bell and double it up. Twist the two wires together so they are even and firm. Whereas the clapper in a real bell swings from side to side, this has to be avoided with these fragile bells, in case some over-enthusiastic bellringer comes along and cracks the shell!

Thread the twisted wire through the hole in the top of the shell and when the height inside the shell is correct, cut the wire, approximately 0.5 cm (¼in) above the hole. Bend the two ends over the shell exterior and glue them in place with a little rapid epoxy glue.

Now I apply the bell handles. These should ideally be made of wood, but I have yet to find a source of supply for these, or a friendly woodturner. You could take a handle off a brass bell, if

Projects

you can find one small enough. However, there are a limited number of designs large and small in gold or silver coloured metal available, and these can be bought from craft shops or egg craft suppliers.

Attach the handle to the top of the shell with more rapid epoxy glue, making sure the bell wires are covered. Set the bell at eye level on a flat surface and turn slowly to check the handle is straight. Adjust if necessary before the glue sets.

Now decide on your decorations. A Christmas transfer adds a festive feel to the shell shown on the right (for the techniques see page 49). Three coats of varnish are then applied over the entire shell and transfer. Allow each coat to dry before applying the next. Bread dough flowers are glued to the other bell, using rapid epoxy, (see page 60).

The next stage is to add the braids and edgings, (see page 44). The lower edge of the dark green bell is trimmed with gold beads, with a row of gold braid bordering each side; a row of gold beads has been placed around the handle where it joins the shell to give a neat finish. The marbled bell is trimmed with wide gold braid, both on the handle on the lower edge. A gold filigree decorates the base of the handle.

Crib

Babies' cribs are an unusual gift for a newborn, or as the decoration on top of the christening cake. I usually make them out of hen or duck eggs, but if you are feeling enthusiastic you can make more elaborate designs with small goose eggs. I'm not much of a needlewoman and would do anything rather than fiddle about with lots of pieces of material, but for those of you who enjoy making dolls' things, you could really go to town with tiny pillows, lace coverlets and a miniature mattress.

Materials

As the shapes and sizes of eggs vary, it is impossible to give exact measurements of the amount of material required.

Rubber band and soft pencil for marking the shell; hacksaw or electric drill, mask and goggles for cutting the egg; blown or whole hen, duck or goose egg; paints; varnish; craft glue; cardboard; cottonwool or thin foam padding; square of white satin; thin lace trimming; length of finely pleated nylon edging approximately 5 cm (2in) deep; frills, ribbons and extra lace for decoration; miniature sleeping baby doll; small plastic curtain ring.

Two duck eggs are used to create these two tiny cribs. The eggs are cut into the crib shape, then covered with lace. Small mattresses are set inside each shell and braids are trimmed down to fit all edges. Two little sleeping babies complete the designs.

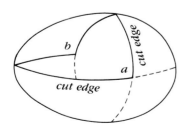

Method

Cut the egg into the crib shape first as shown here. First mark out your guidelines using the rubber band as a guide, mark out the first guideline horizontally around the shell with the pencil, making two equal halves. Remove the band and turning the shell so that the fattest end is at the top, place it about one-third of the way down the egg, repeating the marking procedure. Rub out the pencil line *a* to *b*, represented by the dotted line in the drawing. This will be the hood and if you don't rub out the line you may forget and cut the hood off!

When you are happy with the guidelines, start cutting. Hold the egg firmly with the thumb along the pencil line and rest your elbows on the table to steady your hands before commencing. When you reach the membrane, slit through it with a craft knife, or razor blade. Wash and dry the shell.

If I use a duck egg I leave it in its natural state of white or pretty blue. Two or three coats of varnish to add strength are all it requires. Otherwise, paint it pink, palest blue or white, but keep it delicate.

81

How you complete the inside and outside is entirely a matter of personal preference. I always start with the inside decorations first.

The inside of the crib can be left plain with one or two coats of white paint, then trimmed with narrow lace edging; measure the amount required, then fix in place with craft glue.

I favour a delicate draped look, which is easily achieved with finely pleated nylon edging, about 5 cm (2in) wide. Place a line of craft glue around the outside cut edge of the crib. Take a length of the nylon edging. Attach the rolled edge of the pleats to the outside edge, level with the top cut edge, starting at the angle of the hood on one side. Do it in stages and continue right round, over the top of the hood, until the edging meets up. Cut off at the exact meeting place. When the glue is dry, fold the material away inside the shell, pushing the pleats back into the hood and down into the bottom of the crib. The mattress will eventually hold all this in place. When you have adjusted the pleats to your liking, a few spots of glue will hold everything in place in the base of the shell. Any surplus material and glue marks will be covered by the mattress, which is the next stage.

Measure the shell circumference halfway down the crib and cut a piece of cardboard that will fit into the shell at this point. This now needs to be covered. I usually use a little cottonwool or thin foam padding topped by a layer of white satin.

Cut out an oval of white satin, approximately 0.5 cm (¼in) larger all round than the cardboard shape. Snip it at 0.5 cm (¼in) intervals around the edge. Place your chosen padding on to the cardboard. Don't make it too thick, just enough to give a soft feel. Make sure the right side of the satin is facing upwards and place the wrong side down on to the padding. Turn the cardboard base, padding and material face down on to your worktop and draw a line of craft glue around the bottom of the base, just inside the edge. When it is becoming tacky, fold the cut satin overlap down on to the sticky edge. Once the satin and padding is secure, put a little glue round the edges of the mattress base, turn it over and press it down into the crib, covering the nylon edging in the base of the shell.

The choice of decoration for the outside is up to you. Most department stores have a wonderful range of frills and lace, some with interwoven fabric and with such a choice you could create a little masterpiece for someone special.

Always try things out to see how they look before actually sticking them on to the shell. Whatever lace you use it needs to be long enough to reach your working surface. If it isn't, use two rows of lace, placing the second row just under the bottom edge of the first one. Start attaching the lace on to the shell at one side next to the hood. Glue the top of the lace so that it meets and touches the edge of the pleated lining. Bring the lace right round, following the line round to the back of the hood. If the lace is stiff enough and the correct length it will support the egg. If, however, the cradle tilts to one side, a small plastic curtain ring fixed to the base will form a stand.

Using the leftover satin, make a tiny pillow to fit into the hood of the crib. Measure out the size required. Cut out two pieces of material, either square or oblong depending on the shape you want, allowing 0.5 cm (¼in) for seams. Lay the two pieces together, right sides facing, and sew around the seam edge on three sides. Turn the pillow right side out, pad with a little cottonwool and oversew the open edge with tiny stitches.

Pink or blue clothed plastic sleeping babies can be bought from most toy shops. By repainting them with acrylic paints and touching up the features, they can look pretty and appealing. Cover the baby with a pretty lace coverlet by cutting a square of lace and hemming each side. Add tiny fancy trimmings to the crib to complete the design.

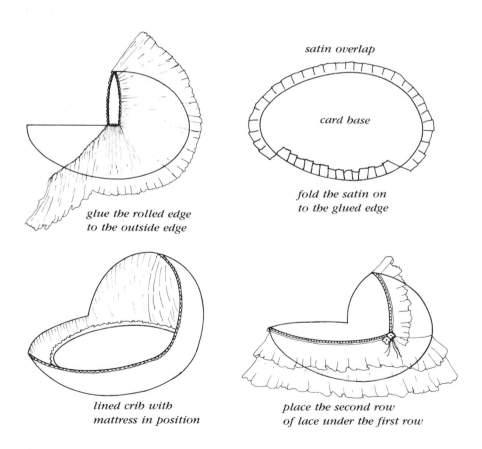

glue the rolled edge
to the outside edge

satin overlap

card base

fold the satin on
to the glued edge

lined crib with
mattress in position

place the second row
of lace under the first row

A goose egg is used to create this green and gold jewel box. The shell is cut about one-third of the way down and then hinged.

Guide lines are drawn on to the shell and then the design is applied, with gesso, through a glue syringe. Once this is dry, the egg is given three coats of matt green enamel. When this is quite dry, the gesso design is picked out in gold paint, using a fine brush. Have a cloth handy to wipe away any brush strokes that stray too far on to the green. Give at least two coats of gold, maybe more depending on the type of paint used. The egg is trimmed with two rows of gold Russian braid around each rim.

As the gilded stand was too bright against the gold design of the egg, I toned it down by painting it with dark brown enamel which was immediately wiped off. This left the residue in all the grooves. You can use this technique with any stand you feel is too bright for your design. Use either enamels or acrylic paints.

Simple jewel box

If you have a choice of shells, choose a goose egg that is long rather than round. Otherwise, any shell will do, even a large hen egg.

Materials

As the shapes and sizes of eggs vary, it is impossible to give exact measurements of the amount of material required.

Blown hen or goose egg; rubber band and pencil for marking the shell; hacksaw or electric craft drill, mask and goggles for cutting the egg; sandpaper; 1 cm (½in) brass hinge; pliers; egg box; sticky tape; super rapid epoxy; cocktail sticks; craft knife or razor blade; tweezers; gesso; matt dark green and gold enamel paints; foil container; plaster, for weighting the shell; cord or braid lining material; craft glue; trace chain (optional); stand.

Method

The cutting line should be on, or just above, the widest part of the shell. In most cases I prefer the more pointed end to be at the top but it is a matter of choice. If the cutting line is below the waist, your egg will look top-heavy. Again there are exceptions to this rule but for this egg, above the waist is better.

Mark the cutting line with the rubber band and pencil, (see page 23 for technique), and draw a cross to enable the two halves to be matched up. Cut the egg, then sand the shell lightly with sandpaper until smooth and wipe away any dust. The next stage is to apply the hinge. For the technique turn to page 38.

On the jewel box illustrated opposite, I have raised the gold design with gesso, (see page 30 for technique). This is the next stage. Draw the design on to your shell, using a soft pencil, making sure it matches where the lid and the base meet. I usually draw my designs freehand, but if you doubt your ability, make a template. Apply five layers of gesso to the shell using a fine paintbrush over the drawn design, allowing each layer to dry before applying the next.

For a rich finish, carefully apply four coats of dark green matt enamel paint to the shell, around the raised gesso design, leaving the design areas unpainted. Remember to allow each coat to dry before applying the next. Once the final coat is dry, apply the gold paint to the design, using a fine paintbrush. If any blobs of gold paint wander on to the green background, wipe off quickly with a damp cloth. Paint over any remaining traces with the green paint.

I always hide cut edges, where I can, with cord or braid. Here I have used two rows of braid top and bottom. Measure the circumference of the shell where the lid meets the base. Cut four lengths of braid. Using craft glue and a cocktail stick, spread a thin line of adhesive, a section at a time, at the very edge of the

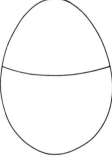

correct cutting line

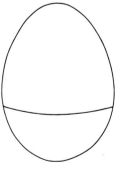

incorrect cutting line

85

shell. When it is tacky, attach the braid. Start at the hinge on one side and work round to the other side of the hinge. Repeat on the other half shell. The second braid should be wide enough to cover the hinge; if not the hinge can be covered with a piece of metal filigree such as half a bell cap, or flat-backed jewels or sequins. A fancy hinge can be left on show.

Always start and end the braid where the join will be least visible, in most cases the hinge area. The two ends of braid should butt together so that the join is virtually invisible. Start the second deeper braid either to the side, or halfway across the hinge. Glue all the way round so that there are no spaces between it and the first row of braid. When you have completed both halves of the shell, close the egg. The braid on both halves should meet all the way round and the egg looks 'whole' again. If they do not, or any fraction of shell edge shows, ease the braid into position with your fingers.

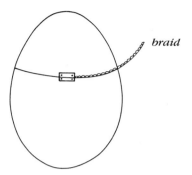

braid

start at the hinge on one side

work round to the other side

attach a second row of wide braid to hide the hinge

A tiny quail's egg makes a lovely little jewel box. The fragile shell is strengthened with four coats of emerald green paint and the interior is lined with contrasting gold mesh.

An oppulent, rather over-the-top egg this! It is a prime example of the egg taking over the design. The final results are far removed from the original concept, which was a simple goose egg, enamelled with stylised flowers and leaves, outlined with gesso. But as each stage progressed, the design seemed to call for something else.

The shell is cut and hinged. The design takes the form of four panels in which the pattern is initially 'drawn' out with gesso. Various coloured enamels are used to paint in the design and gold braid is used to section off each panel.

The egg is satin-lined and is heavily braided around both inside and outside edges. A gold and ruby-red crown adorns the top of the egg, surrounded by gold-set crystals. The finished design sits on a brass and onyx stand.

Now it is time to weight and line the egg. If a trace chain is required, this should be fitted after the lining is in position. The final stage is fixing your jewel box egg to a stand. All these techniques can be found on pages 64–67.

These instructions are basic to all egg designs of this type. Once you have mastered these techniques, you are well on the way to creating your own special designs.

Photograph album

I made this egg as a wedding present for my niece. It really is not too difficult if it survives the cutting. Be patient and handle each cut piece with great care; the thin slices of shell are so easily broken.

Materials

As the shapes and sizes of eggs vary, it is impossible to give exact measurements, or the amount of materials required.

Blown goose egg; sandpaper; elastic band and soft pencil for marking the shell; hacksaw or electric craft drill, mask and goggles, for cutting the shell; matt enamel paints; stiff card; eight photographs; craft glue and epoxy rapid glue; gold braid and cord; small hinges; plastic lemonade bottle; trimmings and decorations; bread dough flowers; cradle stand.

A beautiful bouquet of miniature bread dough flowers is set into a lace-covered shell showcase and the whole egg opens up to reveal a treasured wedding album.

This exquisite design is not too difficult to attempt, as long as each cut out section is handled with care.

Method

With this design I find it is better to sand down the shell, in preparation for painting, before cutting out the sections, because they are so fragile, (see page 33). After sanding, lay the egg horizontally on the work surface, and using the rubber band and pencil, mark the first guide line around the centre of the shell. Measure the distance from the centre line to the tip of the egg on each side, then divide each half into three equal sections. You will now have six sections. Remember to handle each piece of shell with extreme care.

The colour scheme for the wedding was apricot and cream, so I painted the exterior of each shell hoop with matt cream enamel. This adds some strength, but until the album is assembled treat each section like glass!

Once the final coat of paint is dry, the next stage is to fit the photographs, with card backing, into the shell pieces. Each shell section can be used as a template. Take the first shell piece and place it on a sheet of stiff card. Draw around it and then repeat, so you have two pieces of card, one for each side of the cut piece. I always use the card from packets of tights or stockings, but any card of the same thickness would do.

Now you have to cut out the egg shaped card and photograph trimmed down to fit inside the shell piece (use the card as a template for the photograph). In the design shown on page 88 I have framed each photograph with thick braid, so if you want to do the same, make allowances for the thickness of braid you will be using when trimming the card and photograph. You will not want it to stand proud of the shell edge so it will not fold up flush, one section with the other.

The piece of card can now be glued into position. Holding this first card in the shell while it sticks is easy enough because you have access from the other side of the shell. Place a line of white glue around the inside of the shell and position the card, holding it in place until it is quite secure. The next piece of card for the opposite side poses more of a problem as it has a habit of falling inwards, and is difficult to retrieve. To overcome this I push a fine hair pin, or piece of doubled up wire, through the centre of the cut out card and bend back the ends of the wire to hold it. This way I can pull the card into position until the glue is dry. When set hard, I remove the wire.

Insert all the pieces of card in this way, remembering to cut out the photographs as you go along. It might help to number them on the back, so that you remember which photograph goes with which section. When all the cards are fixed, place a spot of craft glue on each photograph and glue into place.

Now each photograph is framed with gold braid. Measure the circumference of each section and cut out lengths of braid to fit. Do not overlap braid edges, or the effect will be clumsy and untidy. Place a thin line of glue around the inside of the shell and attach the braid.

The bottom of the egg is left plain in this design, but I cut out a window in the top of the shell, (see page 30 for technique). I made a tiny bouquet of bread dough flowers and painted them in the wedding colours, then placed them in the window, covering them with a plastic dome. The finished egg can be seen on page 89; it illustrates the window beautifully.

The whole egg is now hinged together using small but firm hinges, with the hinges placed halfway down each section and on alternate sides of the assembled shell, (see page 38 for technique). Check with the illustration before placing each hinge.

Hinge the first two sections together. Ensure the two sections meet perfectly when folded together, checking and adjusting before the glue sets hard. Leave for an hour or two before adding the next section, placing the hinge exactly opposite the first hinge on the alternate side. Continue with the rest of the sections in the same manner.

To add a lovely finishing touch, I have added a wide braid edged with fine cord to the outside of the two centre frames. This covers the hinges and adds strength to the two most fragile pieces of the shell. The other two sections are trimmed with cord. Measure your cord and braid in the usual way, then attach to the shells with craft glue.

Each hinge is covered with tiny gold metal leaves. Attach these with glue, making sure it does not drip on to the hinge post – or the hinge will not open!

The bouquet in the window is framed with looped braid, which is measured and attached in the usual way and a pearl drop earring adds a pretty touch. It is glued to the centre edge of the top section with glue to form a pull.

The folded egg is laid in a cradle stand. This is one occasion where you do not glue the egg to the stand.

Sleeping Beauty

This design is comprised of several straight cuts. It has always reminded me of a canopied bed and I turned this idea around in my mind for two years before the idea of Sleeping Beauty emerged. I sketched it out on paper with a list of items I would need, what I could make and where compromises would have to be made. I was very satisfied with the final result, although it was not quite the same as my original idea.

Materials

As the shapes and sizes of eggs vary, it is impossible to give exact measurements of the amount of material required.

Large fat blown goose egg; rubber band, soft pencil and rubber for marking the shell; hacksaw or electric craft drill for cutting the egg; sandpaper; craft glue and rapid epoxy glue; odds and ends of fabric, braid, cord and trimmings; scissors; 4 small hinges; acrylic paints; round metal butterfly clips; gesso; green and gold enamel paints; bread dough, (see page 61 for recipe), or modelling clay; miniature bed (sponge foam disc covered with satin and lace); prince and princess (miniature boy and girl doll to scale); bark, ivy leaves and dried foliage for the base.

Method

Find the exact top and bottom of the egg; divide the shell into four equal sections, using the rubber band and pencil, (see page 23 for technique). To mark the canopy place the band around the top of the shell rather less than a third of the way down. Draw in the cutting line. Repeat at the bottom of the egg, leaving enough shell to form the base of the bed. To avoid separating the canopy from the base when cutting, use a soft rubber and erase top and bottom lines between two of the vertical lines in one quarter section only. This section is the back of the bed which joins the canopy to the base. The sections you are cutting out are around the middle of the egg, so rub out all other unwanted lines on the canopy and base. Score around all the remaining cutting lines, then start cutting around the top, bottom, then the lines on each side of the back, (see page 23 for technique). Keep all pieces of shell safe in a box when not working with them.

The shell is now in two parts. Take the section that has been removed and number the marked areas, 1, 2 and 3, *before* cutting and separating them. If you don't do this the pieces could easily become mixed up at a later stage. Cut this section into three, then cut the middle section in half to form the castle doors.

The inside of the egg needs to give the impression of an old castle room, rich but slightly faded. I used some old brocade, heavily embroidered with metallic black and gold thread, for the 'walls'. Choose a suitable material and cut out pieces a little larger

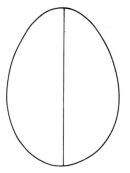

pencil lines quartering the shell

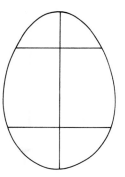

guide lines top and bottom of shell

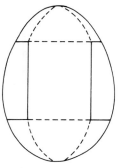

rub out top and bottom lines on one quarter section

While Sleeping Beauty dreams the years away beneath her lace-covered canopy, the handsome prince battles his way through the tangled forest ... this lovely design captures a feeling of fairytale romance on a miniature scale and recreates the story in a charming three dimensional way.

than each of the four pieces of shell you have just cut out plus the back wall in the main shell.

If the material is patterned, it must follow through all the inside walls. This is a little tricky, but is easier if the shell pieces are laid out in order, right way up. Work from left to right and glue the bits of material on to the insides of the shells with craft glue. Don't forget the fixed main wall. Smooth each piece well into the curve of the shell and out to the edge and when dry trim all round the edges with small sharp scissors, flush with the shell edge. To neaten edges use braid and cord. Measure the lengths required and attach with craft glue. In my design I used a deep braid at the bottom, rather like a skirting board, a more delicate looped trim for the top and then gold cord was run down each side to cover any rough edges.

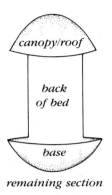

remaining section

The next stage is applying the hinges, (see page 38 for technique). Starting at the back, put section 1 back into place, adjacent to the fixed back section. Secure it with sticky tape attached to the top and bottom of the shell. If the 'doors' tend to drop inwards during this process, screw up a little tissue paper and place it in the shell for support. When the first hinge is secure and working freely, leave the sticky tape on and continue with the opposite side, hinging on section '3'. Leave it taped in position. Using exactly the same procedure, hinge on the left and right side of the front doors, attaching them to sections 1 and 3.

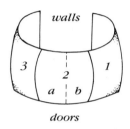

doors

Using acrylic paints, paint the outside, except for the doors and roof, to represent stones; cover the hinges with fairly thick paint so that they integrate with the rest of the stonework. Paint the doors to look like heavy wood planks, with black 'cast iron' hinges. The door handles are round metal butterfly clips; paint them black, then when they are dry spread the flat pieces and glue on to the doors with craft glue. The lines and studs on the roof are built up with gesso, (see page 30 for technique). If you want the same effect, draw the lines and circles on to the shell with pencil, then apply several layers of gesso over the design to the thickness required. When the gesso is dry, paint the entire roof area. I used one coat of matt dark green enamel followed by two coats of gold. If you don't want to use this form of decoration, just paint the flat surface of the roof as described.

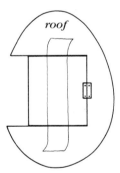

secure door with sticky tape while attaching hinge

Now paint the inside of the roof gold with two layers of gold enamels before going on to the next step, which is to make the four bedposts. I made these with bread dough, (see page 61 for recipe). As this tends to shrink, make the posts extra long and trim off when dry. All bread dough items must be left to air-dry for several days in a warm place before painting and varnishing, so you may prefer to use modelling clay, which is available from most craft shops. This dries faster and some clays can be bought already coloured.

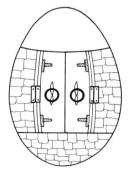

paint the shell to represent stones

With the flat of your hand roll out long thin strips of dough and twist together like barley sugar sticks. Cut off a length to fit from just inside the canopy, to just inside the base. When all the posts are quite dry, paint them with acrylics. Allow to dry before applying one coat of varnish to add strength. When the posts are finally dry, glue them into the egg. Use rapid epoxy, attaching the back posts to the inside of the rear fixed panel, one on each side. Line up the front posts with those at the back; glue each one inside the canopy at the top and down into the base. Then glue a strip of braid around the inside edge of the base. Finish off the canopy by fixing a deep loop braid around the inside edge of the top shell.

The bed is made from a satin and lace covered foam sponge disc. Set this into the shell base and lay the princess on top. I made my princess and prince out of modelling clay, but a tiny doll dressed in satin and lace would look just as effective. As a final touch, a few cobwebs made from wisps of Christmas 'angel hair' are pulled across the walls.

I found the bark base and strips of young ivy whilst walking in the woods. You can of course buy cork bark from most florists, but it is much cheaper to find your own. I always wash off any pieces of wood I find before preserving them. When the bark is dry, apply several coats of white wood glue. As well as preserving the wood, it fixes any loose bits and also gives it a shiny finish. Glue the egg on to the bark, using plenty of rapid epoxy to make sure it is secure. Any glue that shows can be covered with ivy or other dried material. The ivy represents the forest surrounding the castle. Twine the strands around the stand and up on to the egg, gluing here and there to make them firm. Finally fix the prince into position with rapid epoxy.

Index

Most of the eggs illustrated in the book are varnished, hinged and edged with braids, cord or jewellery, so these applications are not shown in the index. Specific applications of other crafts are listed under their headings.

If readers have difficulty obtaining any of the materials or equipment mentioned in this book, please write for further information to the publishers.

If you are interested in any other of the art and craft titles published by Search Press please send for free colour catalogue to: Search Press Limited, Dept B, Wellwood, North Farm Road, Tunbridge Wells, Kent TN2 3DR